A BOOK OF BEGINNINGS

A Book of
BEGINNINGS

COMPILED BY JOHN QUINN

VERITAS

Published 2019 by
Veritas Publications
7–8 Lower Abbey Street
Dublin 1, Ireland

publications@veritas.ie
www.veritas.ie

ISBN 978 1 84730 912 9

A catalogue record for this book is
available from the British Library.

Book design by Lir Mac Cárthaigh
Printed in Ireland by
Anglo Printers Ltd, Drogheda

*Veritas books are printed on paper
made from the wood pulp of managed
forests. For every tree felled, at least
one tree is planted, thereby renewing
natural resources.*

'Everything Is Going to Be All
Right' by Derek Mahon (p. 248)
from *New Selected Poems* (2015) and
'The Blind Poet's Vision of Spring'
by Michael Coady (p. 138) from
Given Light (2017), reproduced by
kind permission of the authors
and The Gallery Press, Loughcrew,
Oldcastle, Co. Meath, Ireland.
www.gallerypress.com

'In the Beginning' by Michael
D. Higgins (p. 251) from *An Arid
Season: New Poems*, Dublin: New
Island, 2004, reproduced by kind
permission of the author.

'Warning' by Jenny Joseph (p. 144)
from *Selected Poems*, Bloodaxe
Books, 1992. Adm by Johnson &
Alcock Ltd.

'Begin' by Brendan Kennelly (p. 174)
from *Familiar Strangers: New &
Selected Poems 1960–2004*, Bloodaxe
Books, 2004. With permission.

Lines from 'The Long Garden' (p.
26) from *Collected Poems*, edited by
Antoinette Quinn (Allen Lane,
2004), and 'New Year (untitled)'
(p. 139) by Patrick Kavanagh,
reproduced by kind permission of
the Trustees of the Estate of the late
Katherine B. Kavanagh, through the
Jonathan Williams Literary Agency.

Dedicated to two great Irishmen whose
ideas and writings were the beginnings
of inspiration for me –

MIKE COOLEY,
engineer and consultant
on work and technology

and

CHARLES HANDY,
writer, broadcaster and
social philosopher

Contents

Introduction

I write this on a momentous day in Irish sport. Shane Lowry, the Co. Offaly golfer, has just won the British Open Championship. The nation rejoices at his victory. Inevitably the media will explore his rise to this pinnacle. When did he first take a golf club in his hands? Who encouraged him? Where did the dream begin?

Beginnings fascinate me. Where does a poem come from? A piece of art? What is the root of a dream? What little acorn became the great oak of a career or a business? Where was the seed of a vocation planted? How do we learn, from infancy to adulthood? What is the beginning of adulthood? What is the beginning of wisdom? How is hope born? Where does love spring from?

Beginnings can be prompt and immediate, as Ewan MacColl tells in his beautiful song 'The First Time Ever I Saw Your Face', or as travel writer Dervla Murphy discovered when she was given a second-hand bicycle for her tenth birthday and immediately resolved to cycle to India one day (which, of course, she did).

Equally, beginnings can be slow and gradual, building to an inevitable outcome. The March to Washington began in 1963 but it was many years later before Martin Luther King's dream of racial equality was realised. Beginnings can take root in an unlikely location. As a young boy, writer and political activist Noam Chomsky was heavily influenced by the discussions he heard at his uncle's news stand in Philadelphia. Or, indeed, an unlikely event may be the source of a life-changing experience. Attending his father's funeral at a rural church in Co. Kildare where his father had ministered caused Charles Handy to reflect on the direction his life was taking and to change drastically that direction.

For many writers, the books encountered in youth revealed other worlds that drew them in, subtly and forcibly. Polly Devlin became determined to leave the darkness behind while exploring the books in the loft of her house. Denis Donoghue discovered 'a world full of magical things' when he was given free rein in a teacher's library. Sometimes, all a beginning demands is encouragement, and musician Johnny McDaid found his in winning the first Pushkin Prize as a twelve-year-old boy: 'I recognised the immense reach of having an idea.' What might seem like an ending is often a beginning. For Nelson Mandela, winning freedom for his people was not unlike climbing a great hill: 'One only finds that there are many more hills to climb.'

John O'Donohue said, 'Beginnings are new horizons that want to be seen.' This book is an attempt to capture those horizons, a collection of beginnings, assembled largely from my own radio archives – the memories and experiences of an array of people that I was fortunate to encounter – plus a selection of writings from sources as varied as Dorothy Day and Frank McCourt. Add a sprinkling of personal experiences and a number of poems that echo beginnings. The entire collection, insightful and intriguing, comprises this book of beginnings and is arranged thematically under twelve headings, such as *The Beginning of …* wisdom, hope, a career, a dream.

The selections will hopefully resonate with the reader's own experience, give an insight into enquiring minds, and maybe offer inspiration to discover new horizons. Lao Tzu said, 'A journey of a thousand miles begins with a single step.' Together, let us take that step!

John Quinn
July 2019

The Beginning of
LIFE

———

'My spirit flew in feathers ...'

Joy is My Name

*Two short poems from WILLIAM BLAKE capture
the sheer joy of infancy.*

———

Infant Joy

'I have no name:
'I am but two days old.'
What shall I call thee?
'I happy am.
'Joy is my name.'
Sweet joy befall thee!

Pretty joy!
Sweet joy but two days old,
Sweet joy I call thee:
Thou dost smile,
I sing the while,
Sweet joy befall thee!

———

The Angel That Presided O'er My Birth

The Angel that presided o'er my birth
Said, 'Little creature, form'd of Joy and Mirth,
'Go love without the help of any Thing on Earth.'

First Light

What is the earliest memory you have? For most of us it would be early days at school but SEAMUS HEANEY could recall a pre-school experience.

———

I'm not sure whether I actually remember it or if people talking about it has given me a picture of it, but my first sense of myself on this planet was when I was 'lost' one afternoon in the field at home in Mossbawn in Co. Derry. I would have been two or three at the time. My mother was worried about me until I was found in the middle of a pea-rig, a rig of peas, and there I was, hidden among the rods. I like to think of that as an image of the womb itself, with the green veins all around me. It was part of a warmish balmy element that you move in as a child, close to parents, with the smell of clothes and adult bodies around you. Also, when my mother found me, I was crying – another image of the moment of birth.

Remembering

A lyrical tribute to the glory of childhood. THOMAS HOOD's much-loved poem 'I Remember, I Remember' celebrates the innocence and joy of childhood and has resonated so much with its readers for over a century and a half. We all remember days when our spirit flew in feathers.

I Remember, I Remember

I remember, I remember
The house where I was born,
The little window where the sun
Came peeping in at morn;
He never came a wink too soon,
Nor brought too long a day,
But now, I often wish the night
Had borne my breath away!

I remember, I remember,
The roses, red and white;
The violets, and the lily-cups,
Those flowers made of light!
The lilacs where the robin built,
And where my brother set
The laburnum on his birthday –
The tree is living yet!

I remember, I remember,
Where I was used to swing;
And thought the air must rush as fresh
To swallows on the wing:
My spirit flew in feathers then,
That is so heavy now,
And summer pools could hardly cool
The fever on my brow!

I remember, I remember,
The fir trees dark and high;
I used to think their slender tops
Were close against the sky:
It was a childish ignorance,

But now 'tis little joy
To know I'm farther off from Heaven
Than when I was a boy.

Becoming

In his poem 'There Was a Child Went Forth' – thought to be autobiographical – WALT WHITMAN describes the child's 'becoming', absorbing all the presences and experiences that are part of his world. A magical process that 'will always go forth every day'.

There Was a Child Went Forth

There was a child went forth every day,
And the first object he look'd upon, that object he
    became,
And that object became part of him for the day or
    a certain part of the day,
Or for many years or stretching cycles of years.

The early lilacs became part of this child,
And grass and white and red morning-glories,
    and white and red clover, and the song of the
    phoebe-bird,

And the Third-month lambs and the sow's pink-
   faint litter, and the mare's foal and the cow's
   calf,
And the noisy brood of the barnyard or by the
   mire of the pond-side,
And the fish suspending themselves so curiously
   below there, and the beautiful curious liquid,
And the water-plants with their graceful flat
   heads, all became part of him.

The field-sprouts of Fourth-month and Fifth-
   month became part of him,
Winter-grain sprouts and those of the light-
   yellow corn, and the esculent roots of the
   garden,
And the apple-trees cover'd with blossoms and
   the fruit afterward, and wood-berries, and the
   commonest weeds by the road,
And the old drunkard staggering home from the
   outhouse of the tavern whence he had lately
   risen,
And the schoolmistress that pass'd on her way to
   the school,

And the friendly boys that pass'd, and the
    quarrelsome boys,
And the tidy and fresh-cheek'd girls, and the
    barefoot negro boy and girl,
And all the changes of city and country wherever
    he went.

His own parents, he that had father'd him and she
    that had covceiv'd him in her womb and birth'd
    him,
They gave this child more of themselves than that,
They gave him afterward every day, they became
    part of him.

The mother at home quietly placed the dishes on
    the supper-table,
The mother with mild words, clean her cap and
    gown, a wholesome odor falling off her person
    and clothes as she walks by,
The father, strong, self-sufficient, manly, mean,
    anger'd, unjust,
The blow, the quick loud word, the tight bargain,
    the crafty lure,

The family usages, the language, the company, the
    furniture, the yearning and swelling heart,
Affection that will not be gainsay'd, the sense of
    what is real, the thought if after all it should
    prove unreal,
The doubts of day-time and the doubts of night-
    time, the curious whether and how,
Whether that which appears so is so or is it all
    flashes and specks?
Men and women crowding fast in the streets, if
    they are not flashes and specks what are they?
The streets themselves and the facades of houses,
    and goods in the windows,
Vehicles, teams, the heavy-plank'd wharves, the
    huge crossing at the ferries,
The village on the highland seen from afar at
    sunset, the river between,
Shadows, aureola and mist, the light falling on roofs
    and gables of white or brown two miles off,
The schooner near by sleepily dropping down the
    tide, the little boat slack-tow'd astern,
The hurrying tumbling waves, quick-broken
    crests, slapping,

The strata of color'd clouds, the long bar of
maroon-tint away solitary by itself, the spread
of purity it lies motionless in,
The horizon's edge, the flying sea-crow, the
fragrance of salt marsh and shore mud,
These became part of that child who went forth
every day, and who now goes, and will always
go forth every day.

The Pockets of God

An ordinary garden where animals rooted and rubbish was dumped became for the young PATRICK KAVANAGH and his peers an imaginary world where anything was possible.

———

FROM The Long Garden

It was the garden of the golden apples,
A long garden between a railway and a road,
In the sow's rooting where the hen scratches
We dipped our fingers in the pockets of God.

In the thistly hedge old boots were flying sandals
By which we travelled through the childhood skies,
Old buckets rusty-holed with half-hung handles
Were drums to play when old men married wives.

The pole that lifted the clothes-line in the middle
Was the flag-pole on a prince's palace when
We looked at it through fingers crossed to riddle
In evening sunlight miracles for men.

The Beginning of

LEARNING

———

'I played with children so that
I could learn from them.'

In the Beginning was Music

During a seminar in Dublin in 1994, the world-renowned violinist ISAAC STERN made an impassioned plea for the place of the arts in the life of a child.

———

Music for me is the most natural form of the arts. Why does it speak so easily to so many people of differing backgrounds and at different times? The answer is simple [*he raps the lectern in heartbeat rhythm*]. While the foetus is still in the womb – the first tempo. And the moment that foetus comes to life – ehhhh! [*he emits a piercing 'baby shriek'*]. Sound, sound and tempo – the basis of music, the most natural form of human expression. Every child reacts to it. Sound, the sound of parents' voices. The sound of caressing, of comfort, of strength. This is what all children respond to and there is no such thing as an ungifted child. They all react. They are all willing to learn …

We have reached what I call the 'digitalisation of the world'. You press buttons for preformed thought. You look at television for preformed opinions. And because of short attention spans and the pressure of advertising space, everything is presented in short bites. Anything that has to do with the quality of life takes time for reflection. Children need that time. The arts part of the curriculum is the beginning of the beginning of that process but it must begin early – in the home and in the school. What kind of life surrounds the child at home? Do parents let the child turn on anything they want on radio or television or do they consciously surround the child in some way with what is part of the beautiful stream of man's creativity? Not in order to force it down the child's throat but to make it a natural happenstance of daily living.

Then comes the school. Some of us come from a European background where no child was considered educated if it didn't play, dance, sing, paint – not to *be* a dancer, singer, painter but to know: to know what is beautiful, to know what is possible. As I travel the world I notice a growing lack of respect for teachers in society. They are not the people to whom we give the greatest accolades or income possibilities. And yet I do not know of any well-educated person for whom somehow, somewhere, one teacher didn't turn a light on inside and make that person become what he/she is today.

Teaching – knowledgeable, informed, enthusiastic, dedicated, absolutely passionate teaching. That is one of the keys to the future. And parents – demanding, voting, caring, loving parents. That is another key. Between the two there can be a new world for the next generations. And we have little time. We have already lost one or two generations because the speed of communications has overcome the respect for learning, the idea that a person of the mind is perhaps more important than the person behind the till.

Natural Learning

MIKE COOLEY is an award-winning engineer, writer and broadcaster. The foundations of his career were laid down during his childhood in Tuam, Co. Galway through his observation of nature.

———

In Tuam as young children we used simply to play with pieces of wood and the game was to pass it round and see what we could envisage in that piece of wood. Some people would see skeletons, and other people would see dragons, and so on. I notice even today when I look at complex pages and pages of mathematical formulae, I somehow still have the capacity to see a pattern in that mass of things. A deep pattern recognition capability was developed at that early stage. We used to play with water in the Ballygaddy river and I remember making little locks and noticing how, as the water approached them, it increased in velocity – you put little ships on it and you could confirm this. I subsequently understood the Venturi phenomenon and its related mathematics that much better precisely because I had gone through that kind of experience.

I learned so much about aerodynamics by watching trees in motion. My early insight into guidance systems was when I wondered how the geese used to come to the west of Ireland about this time each year – the third week in October – and how they had guided themselves from Canada and Siberia.

There was a sense in which one could see the greatness of nature, and one began to understand that we had to accord with it. I think people used to say *Ní hé lá na gaoithe, lá na scolb* ('The windy day is not the day for thatching'), which means that you actually mould what you're doing partly to accord with nature. It is most important that we look at other cultures and other ways of viewing these relationships. There's the great saying from the North American Indian when his people were rounded up in the compound:

I say to you my people, the paleface will take the eagle from the sky, he will take

the salmon from the streams, he'll take the
buffalo from the plains, he'll poison the air
that we breathe and the water that we drink.

Everything Catches

SHINICHI SUZUKI pioneered a very successful system for teaching music to young children. It was modelled on the way children acquired their mother tongue. 'Everything catches,' he argued. His inspiration came from reading Tolstoy's Diary.

———

I consider that seventeen was the age at which my foundations were laid. In a manner of speaking it was the year I was born, the year I emerged as a human being ... I went into a bookstore and looked around some books on a shelf at random. After some time fate led me to a copy of Tolstoy. It was the small *Tolstoy's Diary*. I casually took it down from the shelf and opened it at random. My eyes fell on the following words, 'To deceive oneself is worse than to deceive others ...'

I had been inflamed by Tolstoy; I had learned to realise how precious children of four or five were, and wanted to become as one of them. They trust people and do not doubt at all. They know only how to love, and know not how to hate. They love justice, and scrupulously keep the rules. They seek joy, and live cheerfully and are full of life. They know no fear, and live in security. I played with children so that I could learn from them. I wanted always to have the meekness of a child. A big revolution took place within me. I feel that this is when the seed was sown of the Talent Education movement that was to be my life-work.

Most of these beautiful children would eventually become adults filled with suspicion, treachery, dishonesty, injustice, hatred, misery, gloom. Why? Why couldn't they be brought up to maintain the beauty of their souls? There must be something wrong with education …

It is in our power to educate all the children of the world to become a little better as people, a little happier. We have to work towards this. I ask no more than the love and happiness of mankind, and I believe that this is what everyone really wants. Love can be had only by loving. Our life is worth living only if we love one another and comfort one another. I searched for that meaning of art in music, and it was through music that I found my work and my purpose in life. Once art to me was something far off, unfathomable and unattainable. But I discovered it was a tangible thing … The real essence of art turned out to be not something high up and far off. It was right inside my ordinary daily self. The very way one greets people and expresses oneself is art. If a musician wants to become a fine artist, he must first become a finer person. If he does this, his worth will appear. It will appear in everything he does, even in what he writes. Art is not in some far-off place. A work of art is the expression of a man's whole personality, sensibility and ability …

My prayer is that all children on this globe become fine human beings, happy people of superior ability, and I am devoting all my energies to making this come about, for I am convinced that all children are born with this potential.

Boarding School – First Night

The experience of boarding school, particularly that first night away from home, can be traumatic. These are my own personal memories (told in the third person) of my first night in Patrician College, Ballyfin, Co. Laois. They are the opening pages of the script of the radio documentary Ballyfin – A Boarding School Memory.

———

There was a giant stone bird sitting on either gate pillar. He would learn later that they were coots, for this was originally the home of the Coote family. It was now Patrician College, Ballyfin Demesne, Portlaoise, Co. Laois – a boarding school for boys. It was September 1954. He was twelve years of age and – holidays apart – this would be his home for the next five years. He was fearful. He had left the familiarity and security of home in a small village in Co. Meath – sixty miles away …

The Ford Prefect rattled over the cattle grid – the first time he had seen a cattle grid. 'Canadian gates' they were called – and they seemed to clang 'Goodbye' – a goodbye to the village, goodbye to his friends, his parents, goodbye to the world …

The avenue was long, winding out of the autumn sunlight, into dark woods and then suddenly into the light again. And there it was – a huge mansion, the biggest he had ever seen. Four great columns guarded the entrance doors where the President stood greeting the parents. The brothers wore long black soutanes with green sashes. He shook hands with the President, Brother Silverius. He would later learn that the boys called him 'Punk'. Brother Silverius said he hoped this young man would be as good as his brother. It was good having a brother in the school already. It helped in the settling in …

They climbed the two flights of stone stairs to the dormitory. On the first landing were the washroom and toilets. He would spend many cold winter mornings in the washroom waiting for a free handbasin for a quick wash before Mass. The dormitory was on the next landing – an L-shaped room with fifty or sixty beds. His brother chose two beds half-way down. The trunk was opened and the starched sheets with his name sewn on the corner were procured. They made up the beds and packed their lockers with clothes and toiletries …

The dormitory grew noisier as more boys arrived. Old boys – anyone in second year or beyond – shouted greetings and swaggered about knowingly. The new boys tried hard to look settled and happy and knowing. And then it was time for his parents to go … He swallowed hard and said goodbye to his father. His mother kissed him – he knew she would miss him, the baby of the family. He fought back the tears and waved goodbye as the car moved down the avenue, around the bend and into the woods.

He awoke to a new and strange world. Brother Angelus marched through the dormitory ringing a hand bell. It was so unusual to find himself sharing a room with sixty other boys. The hubbub and clamour grew as the washroom filled up and boys queued up for handbasins. He washed quickly. The towel smelled of home. He buried his face in it, wishing that smell would linger … His brother told him to hurry. The day proper began as every day would begin – with Mass in the Oratory.

Father Phelan came in from Ballyfin village to say Mass. The juniors knelt at the front of the Oratory. He himself was right under the huge fireplace which was now boarded up. Each seat had a series of white enamel numbers affixed to it. Later he would learn how to unscrew the number with a nail file, insert a message behind the number and screw it back on. In this way he would be remembered in fifty years' time, maybe forever …

He thought of the many times he had served Mass in his home village, the dark winter mornings when the frost pinched his face on the way to the church. He would gladly exchange that for this bright September morning. He wondered what his parents were doing now … his mother probably at Mass praying for him … his father stoking the range … Roy the dog waiting to be released from his kennel. He wished he was at home …

That First Day

In his conversations with Dennis O'Driscoll for the book Stepping Stones, *SEAMUS HEANEY recalls his first days at school.*

My memory of learning to read goes back to my first days in Anahorish School, the charts for the letters, the big-lettered reading books. I cried on the first morning I went to school, of course. My father was shaving, getting ready to go to the fair. Phil McNicholl, a girl a year or two older than me who lived just beyond the carpenter's house, had the job of bringing me but I let up the bawl the minute she came to the door and my father had to pretend to be angry – although it didn't seem like pretence then. I went off very sorrowfully. When we got near the school, I was surprised to see so many children running about the place at that time of the morning, then the old breadcrumby smell of the porch, the bareness and extent of the rows of coat hangers. I remember also being embarrassed about my schoolbag – it wasn't new and it wasn't strictly speaking a schoolbag. Something better, maybe, but it wasn't what others had, so it bothered me. It was a hand-made leather shoulder pouch, the kind of thing bus conductors used to collect fares in; it had belonged to my uncle Peter, I think, who drove a bread cart and had to have a shoulder bag for his money. What I liked best about those first days, I have to say, was being taken care of by Phil, having a special closeness to her. First love, I suppose.

First Day at School

ELIZABETH SHANE's poem 'Wee Hughie' has touched many a heart over the years.

———

He's gone to school, Wee Hughie
An' him not four.
Sure I saw the fright was in him
When he left the door.

But he took a hand o' Denny
An' a hand o' Dan,
Wi' Joe's owld coat upon him –
Och, the poor wee man!

He cut the quarest figure,
More stout nor thin:
An' trottin' right and steady
Wi' his toes turned in.

I watched him to the corner
O' the big turf stack,
An' the more his feet went forrit,
Still his head turned back.

He was lookin'
Would I call him –
Och me heart was woe –
Sure it's lost I am without him,
But he be to go.

I followed to the turnin'
When they passed it by,
God help him, he was cryin',
An' maybe, so was I.

Genius

I am constantly lost in admiration for the linguistic genius that is the young child. The apparent ease with which the child acquires language belies the amount of creativity, improvisation, imitation, guesswork and sheer hard work the child puts into the task. It is just a joy to listen to them play with sounds and adapt words to their own world. My six-year-old granddaughter, Riley, wanted to play a game with her mother who tried to explain that they didn't have the required materials. With a shrug of her shoulders, Riley replied, 'We can improvise ...'

KORNEI CHUKOVSKY was a much-loved children's poet who spent a lifetime observing and recording how children acquired and developed language. In his book From Two to Five, *he describes the child as 'a linguistic genius' and a 'tireless explorer' who is relentless in the discovery of the world of language.*

It is frightening to think what an enormous number of grammatical forms are poured over the poor head of the young child. And he, as if it were nothing at all, adjusts to all this chaos, constantly sorting out into rubrics the disorderly elements of the words he hears, without noticing, as he does this, his gigantic effort. If an adult had to master so many grammatical rules within so short a time, his head would surely burst – a mass of rules mastered so lightly and so freely by the two-year-old 'linguist'. The labour he thus performs at this age is astonishing enough, but even more amazing and unparalleled is the ease with which he does it. In truth, the young child is the hardest mental toiler on our planet. Fortunately, he does not even suspect this.

Starting with an A

Imagine! Imagine you are a student at the New England Conservatory of Music in Boston. Serious stuff. It is the beginning of the college year. The professor breezes in and in the course of his address he announces that he is giving an A to each student. At the beginning of the year! Imagine! The professor is BEN ZANDER. There is, however, just one condition attached to the award of an A.

Sometime during the next two weeks the students must write a letter dated the end of the school year, which begins with the words, 'Dear Mr Zander, I got my A because ...'

The students must place themselves in the future, looking back on all the insights and milestones they have attained during the year. Everything must be written in the past tense. Ben Zander is interested in the person that each student will have become – in their attitudes, feelings and world view. Each student must 'fall passionately in love' with the person described in that letter. It is all a matter of possibility.

Giving the A is a very subtle and a very liberating approach. It is not – Zander claims – falsely building up students, but speaking to them in a way that enables them to be the best they can be. It is not about boasting of your achievements but about raising your self-esteem. It enables you to see all of who you are and be all of who you are without having to resist or deny any part of yourself. It avoids what Zander calls the 'downward spiral' – the negative thinking that says things are not possible, thus breeding cynicism and extinguishing passion.

Ben Zander draws inspiration from Michelangelo's concept that inside each block of stone or marble there dwells a beautiful statue. 'If we were to apply this visionary concept to education,' he says, 'it would be pointless to compare one child to another. Instead, all the energy would be focused on chipping away at the stone, getting rid of whatever is in the way of each child's developing skills, mastery and self-expression.' For the teacher, this innovative approach 'transports your relationship from the world of measurement into the universe of possibility'.

Giving an A can be applied to any relationship or any walk of life. It is not restricted to an elite of gifted students of music. 'The A is not an expectation to live up to but a possibility to live into.' It is about keeping that door of enthusiasm open (remembering that enthusiasm means 'full of God') – enthusiasm that each of us had as children. We need to come from the power of children, Zander argues.

The Lost City

In the 1930s foreign travel was the stuff of dreams for most Irish people. For the few, a boat trip to Liverpool or the Isle of Man would have been the summit of exotica. Imagine, then, the delight of a cruise to Rome for a young Dublin boy. That boy was JAMES PLUNKETT, who went on a Holy Year pilgrimage to Rome with one thousand five hundred other boy scouts. Rome was indeed magical, but Pompeii was unforgettable.

One morning in March of 1934, instead of wandering along the river wall watching the ships sailing off to foreign places, I myself stood aboard a ship and saw all the familiar landmarks gliding past me as quietly as if it were a dream.

The ship was the *SS Lancastria* and we were to see – in addition to Rome – a little bit of Spain, a little bit of Gibraltar, the town of Ceuta in North

Africa with its Foreign Legion (Spanish) barracks, Naples and beside Naples – the part of the journey I was to remember the most vividly – Pompeii, the ancient town dominated by the volcanic Mount Vesuvius.

One morning in AD 79 that volcano, after behaving itself impeccably for centuries, suddenly burst into frenzied activity, catching the people of Pompeii unawares. For three days it poured tons of cinders and ashes and pumice stone on the city. Day was turned into night, thousands of people were trapped by pouring lava while others only escaped by dropping everything they were doing and fleeing away. The volcanic ash buried the city completely, so completely indeed that in time people almost forgot it had ever been there. It was all of one thousand seven hundred years later when the historians decided to set about digging it out again bit by bit.

And that's how it came about that my friends and I were able to walk its streets nearly two thousand years after it had been destroyed. For one romantic-minded young boy the experience was unforgettable. We walked the streets and looked at the walls of its houses; we even saw the charred remains of the nuts and fruits and loaves of bread that the people had left behind when they fled to escape the lava and the terrible rain of fire. We walked by the wine shops and examined the sentry boxes used by guards; we saw the deep ruts worn in the paved stone of the roadways by the traffic of chariot wheels. And, to bring it all up to date, on a flagstone outside the gate of one of the houses were carved the words: *Cave Canem* which we had enough schoolboy Latin to be able to translate: Beware of the dog.

There were grim remains too; a soldier stretched in death at his post whom the ash had coated thickly and transformed into a stone statue; a dog too, to which the same thing had happened. It lay with its legs bunched up and its neck twisted to one side in a last agony.

That visit awed me as much in memory as it did in actuality and inspired a schoolboy poem – a sonnet, no less:

I walked in old Pompeii when the sun
dipped westward and bent to bid adieu
Saw old Vesuvius raise himself to view
The mute remaining of an age undone;
Still line on shattered line the houses run
A silenced theatre tier on tier where drew
Poets the dreams they wrought, the tale
    anew
(Shadows by erstwhile shadows shadow
    spun)
And all was still. Along the dusty ways
No spectre moved, no stirring of the grass
Rimming each creviced flag, no legions
    march;
A sundial sits to stare the passing days
And no one notes. The swift years pass
And Time broods silent in a broken arch.

As verse it has its shortcomings, but it triggers off the excitement and awe of that walk down the streets of history even today.

The Beginning of
LOVE

———

'A vision in a black leather coat.'

The First Time Ever I Saw Your Face (1)

This great modern love song was written by folk singer EWAN MacCOLL for his then girlfriend and later wife, PEGGY SEEGER. During the course of a long interview with them in 1987, they told me how the song had come about.

———

Peggy: About 1956 I was on a sabbatical from Radcliffe College in the USA, trekking around Europe playing my music. I was in Denmark when I got a phone call from London from folk music collector Alan Lomax. He needed a female singer/banjo player for a television series, *Dark of the Moon*. When I arrived in London he told me that he really needed me for a new singing group he was forming. I had been travelling for twenty-six hours and looked a mess in jeans. Alan's girlfriend, a posh model, literally scrubbed me clean, gave me one of her dresses, a fantastic hairdo, makeup and high heels, so when I tottered into the studio, that was the first time ever Ewan saw me … Poor Ewan fell in love with this vision.

Ewan: It wasn't the vision, it was the banjo!

Peggy: About a year later I was on a solo tour in America and urgently needed new material – a love-song that would last one minute, twenty-five seconds! So Ewan wrote this song and sang it to me over the phone.

Ewan: The only time I ever sang it!

Peggy: I remember writing it down because it was difficult to remember. It is almost classical folksong tradition – The first time … The first time … The first time – each verse taking the courtship further. It got instant reaction and became a huge hit and has been interpreted in many ways. But I hold that no one sings it as well as I do, because I understand it in the folk-song manner. It's a simple lyric melody like an unaccompanied Irish song.

First Date

What memories, what emotions do those words 'first date' arouse in you? Excitement? Pride? Nervousness? Disappointment? For MAEVE BINCHY, it was all those things in that order, culminating in total shame.

When I say that I didn't have any boyfriends at the age of fifteen it was certainly by accident, not by design. I would have been delighted to have had boyfriends but there weren't many opportunities. I didn't have any older brothers. My brother was eight years younger than me and he was no use at all in providing companions. I suppose I did meet fellows at parties, but we were very late developers in our era. In the early fifties the whole idea of twelve-year-olds having boyfriends was just unheard of; but at fifteen the latent stirrings were there all right, although they were stirring a bit in vain for me. If you were going to be a saint, you didn't think in terms of a 'sex life', but you did

The Beginning of Love / 59

think in terms of a good, warm honest Christian marriage: I did hope that I would get around to that.

When I was about sixteen the first opportunity came my way. Dún Laoghaire on Saturday afternoons was a great place for parading up and down – like the Italian *passeggiata*. We all used to go to the pictures in Dún Laoghaire on Saturday and look with envy at the people who had fellows – I would always be with my sisters or other girls. However, eventually a boy asked me if I would go to the film *Roman Holiday* with him. I was thrilled. I mentioned casually about eighteen hundred times during the week that I was going to the pictures with him on the Saturday. I felt that at last I had joined the gang. He rang the night before to confirm the date. 'I'll see you inside,' he said. Oh, the shame and the disappointment! Even now, all these years later, I'd like to get hold of him and beat his stupid, thick head against the wall.

The First Time Ever I Saw Your Face (2)

Today is 1 March 2019. It is my birthday! I am fifty-three years old. Well, yes, *chronologically* I am much older than that (throw in another quarter of a century, give or take) – but today is my *real* birthday. Life really began for me fifty-three years ago. Let me take you back to 1 March 1966 …

I am a young teacher but for the past three months I have been a patient in a sanatorium in Blanchardstown, Co. Dublin. I have TB, detected by a mobile x-ray unit that came to University College, Dublin, where I was attending night classes. A rather disruptive experience initially, but once accepted it evolved into a fairly boring routine of rest, medication, rest and more rest. Not a lot happened to disturb the tenor of life in 'the Blanch', as we served out our nine-month 'sentence'. Not until this grey March day.

I have been sent to the main hospital building for some routine tests. My main concern today is that the great racehorse Arkle is running in the Leopardstown Chase this afternoon and I must get to a television set, or at least a radio, to learn of his fate. I am engaged in this quest when an ambulance disgorges a number of female patients outside. I am stopped in my tracks when out steps a vision dressed in a black leather coat. Tall, blonde, elegant, with the walk of a queen. Stunningly beautiful. Where has this ethereal presence come from?

The next thirty minutes are lost in a rather beautiful haze as I am caught between my Arkle quest and the mystery of the vision in a black leather coat. Yes, Arkle did win (but only by a short head) and in my frantic search for a radio, I failed to hold the door open for the vision … Doomed forever? But I did hear her name being called – Miss McKeever. I was more than mildly smitten with Miss McKeever.

In the days that followed I tapped into every information source available and established that she was Olive McKeever, from Co. Meath – very bright, speaks several languages, worked for Aer Lingus and Cunard Shipping Line. Certainly doomed now. Out of my league, surely? But I would be brave and write to her. (No mobile phones in 1966.) In German! To impress the lady. Well, in bog-German, to be exact: *Ich komme aus Co. Meath, genau wie sie*. Cringe material. And just to be sure – in English also. Next came the problem of having the letters smuggled into Unit 5, Ward 2, across the field. (This was 1966, remember.)

Praise the Lord, she replied. The letters flew back and forth until we actually met at Mass in the hospital chapel on Easter Sunday morning, 10 April 1966. Subsequent 'dates' at bingo and film shows and a continuing torrent of letters brought us closer together. I couldn't believe my luck. And then on a bright May evening, we 'escaped' for an hour for a walk through Blanchardstown woods, which included seventeen laps of the boiler house green. It was the most wonderful day of my life up to then.

What more can I say about Olive McKeever? Reader, I married her in Trim church on 18 September 1968 and we were together for thirty-three years until she died suddenly swimming in the sea at Rosslare, Co. Wexford in 2001.

It's a wonderful story. And it all began when a vision in a black leather coat came between me and my equine hero. Happy Birthday to me, indeed.

When First I Saw

As evidenced by his enormous poetic output and his notoriety as a lover, ROBERT BURNS experienced the 'beginning of love' many times. Here he records his feelings for 'fair Jeanie'.

Chorus: She's aye, aye sae blithe, sae gay,
She's aye sae blithe and cheerie,
She's aye sae bonnie, blithe and gay,
O gin I were her dearie!

When first I saw fair Jeanie's face,
I coundna tell what ail'd me:
My heart went fluttering pit-a-pat,
My een they almost fail'd me.
She's aye sae neat, sae trim, sae tight,
All grace does round her hover!
Ae look depriv'd me o' my heart,
And I became her lover.

Had I Dundas's whole estate,
Or Hopetoun's wealth to shine in;

Did warlike laurels crown my brow,
Or humbler bay entwining;
I'd lay them a' at Jeanie's feet,
Could I but hope to move her,
And, prouder than a belted knight,
I'd be my Jeanie's lover.

But sair I fear some happier swain,
Has gain'd sweet Jeanie's favour,
If so, my every bliss be hers,
Though I maun never have her!
But gang she east, or gang she west,
'Twixt Forth and Tweed all over,
While men have eyes, or ears, or taste,
She'll always find a lover.

Glossary:

aye – always	ae – one
sae –so	sair – sorely
gin – if only	maun – must
een – eyes	gang – go

The Beginning of
A DREAM

'To catch the roaming wind
of the Creative Spirit.'

The Cry of a Child

Alexandra Hamilton, Duchess of Abercorn – known to most as SACHA ABERCORN – lived at Baronscourt, Co. Tyrone through the height of the Troubles in Northern Ireland. When her daughter began to have nightmares about impending violence, Sacha reacted by setting up the Pushkin Trust, which would bring children together from both sides of the religious and border divides in pursuit of the creative spirit through writing, art, dance and environmental study. For over thirty years the Pushkin movement has flourished and grown through the dedicated work of teachers under the pioneering guidance of Sacha, who died in 2018.

———

The work of the Pushkin Trust was born out of a deep sense of outrage that I felt as a mother seeing the damage that was being perpetrated on our children in Northern Ireland in the seventies and eighties, by the destructive powers of bitterness, anger, fear, hatred and terror that had been unleashed. I realised that this brutalising power, if left to its own devices, would damage and distort the natural growth path of our children and history would continue to repeat itself.

The spirit of my ancestor Alexander Pushkin provided us with the initial impetus to lift ourselves out of the tribal experience that divides and separates us, into the realm of the Universal where we all connect as human beings. The Pushkin movement that has grown from that initial response to the 'cry of the child' is not an institution or a corporation but more a kind of sail that we have hitched to catch the roaming wind of the Creative Spirit. No one can touch that wind, but we can feel it; we cannot tie it down, yet we can allow ourselves to be carried by it, bringing out new perspectives as we are lifted beyond the anxieties and pre-occupations of everyday life.

The cloth of Pushkin's sail is woven from fairy tale and myth that speak to us by way of metaphor and symbol. These symbols reverberate in our ears and in our hearts long after the one who has aired them is silent. Ireland and Russia are both nations alive with symbolic meaning and utterance. They have both withstood many attempts to have these symbols usurped for purposes of power and pride.

Even the little stone in the corner of the meadow tells a story. It is a story older than ourselves, of suffering and exposure beyond our imagination, of forces now invisible yet active under our feet. It invites us to think about who we are when we walk past.

The cloth of Pushkin's sail is maintained by our longing for expression, our longing to be listened to. It is ennobled by the kindness and compassion of human encounter.

There is a great wind gathering over Ireland. The spirit is whispering to us as it touches our skin. The faintest form of this wind is the human voice. We breathe it in deeply and it resides for a lingering moment in our lungs, endowing us with the miracle of life, flowing to every cell of our body. From here it leaves us again. If we so wish, it leaves us with a voice. We find words of joy or words of sorrow – we are the sail in that wind, the voice of that breath. We are what we exhale with that life force and we rest in the knowledge that the next intake of breath will follow until our days are ended.

The Landing of the Eagle

On Sunday, 20 July 1969, around the world, huge audiences watch an amazing story unfold through grainy images on television. Then at 20:17, a voice comes from afar: 'The Eagle has landed.' Man has set foot on the moon. For the crew of *Apollo II*, MICHAEL COLLINS, BUZZ ALDRIN and NEIL ARMSTRONG, what was science fiction has become reality. It is both the culmination of years of scientific research and planning – and the beginning of a new era of the exploration of outer space.

When the module landed Buzz Aldrin, an elder of the Presbyterian Church, took communion from a chalice prepared by his pastor.

Neil Armstrong began his descent from the lunar module. On the ladder he uncovered a plaque signed by the astronauts and President Nixon and stating, 'Here men from the planet earth first set foot upon the moon, July 1969, A.D. We came in peace for all mankind.' At 2:56 on 21 July, Armstrong stepped off the ladder with the historic words, 'That's one small step for man, one giant leap for mankind.'

Aldrin joined him on the lunar surface, where they spent over two hours exploring the 'magnificent desolation' (as Aldrin described it) and collecting soil samples. In all, the two spent nearly a full day on the moon before rejoining Michael Collins in the mothership. They would return to earth three days later as heroes. In a television broadcast before they splashed down in the Pacific Ocean, Aldrin reflected, 'This has been far more than three men on a mission to the moon; more still than the efforts of a government and industry team; more even than the efforts of one nation. We feel that this stands as a symbol of the insatiable curiosity of all mankind to explore the unknown. Personally, in reflecting on the events of the past several days, a verse from the Psalms (8:3–4) comes to mind: "When I consider the heavens, the work of thy fingers, the moon and the stars which thou hast ordained; what is man that thou art mindful of him?"'

GRAND AMBITION

As children, we dream great and wonderful dreams. We hope to achieve the celebrity status of the sport or music stars we admire or to emulate the heroes and heroines we read of or see on our screens. In my distant childhood my great ambition was to win the Wimbledon title that had eluded my hero Ken Rosewall. Failing that, I would definitely lead the Meath football team to All-Ireland glory just like the great 'Man in the Cap' Peter McDermott. MAEVE BINCHY had an even greater ambition.

I wanted to be a saint. This was not just a childhood ambition: I wanted to be a saint until I was about twenty-two. It wasn't a question of 'I hope it will happen to me'; I was quite convinced that I would be a saint.

I had a very special relationship with God. I regarded him as a friend, and Irish, and somebody who knew me well. He had sent particular tortures my way – like not being good at games and being fat at school. It was bad, very bad, to be fat, so these were the tortures that God was sending to try me. It was all very clear to me.

But I was hoping against hope that I wouldn't see a vision. People who saw visions very often ended up as martyrs; and although I was dead keen to be a saint, I wanted to be a non-martyred saint. Because of all the stories I had heard about the children of Fatima seeing Our Lady in a tree, I always kept my eyes down on the road if I was walking anywhere with lots of trees. No visions for me! I had worked out this sainthood very well. You didn't have to be a martyr; you didn't even have to be a nun and devote your whole life to sanctity. You just had to have a special relationship with God and be a sort of intermediary between him and the rest of the world.

I worried a lot about people who didn't keep up their own religion. I had a friend whose father was a Protestant – a lovely man whom we all adored because he used to give us four-penny ice creams when every other father only gave us two-penny ones. He used to drive his wife and children to Mass and then go for a walk on Dún Laoghaire pier. I would spend hours with his daughter wondering if he would be damned and roasted in hell. I felt that if he wasn't converted to Catholicism (which would be the ideal thing) he should at least be going to his own church (which would naturally not be as good as the real thing). Imagine this poor unfortunate man being harangued by his eight-year-old daughter and her friend saying, 'Honestly, Mr —, have you thought about it – the devil and the pain that goes on forever?' The more I look back on it, the more I realise what a poisonous little person I was – and having an overdeveloped imagination didn't help.

Part of the sainthood thing, too, was becoming a Child of Mary. This involved a combination of being in a sodality – a religious group – and being a prefect in school. You couldn't become a Child of Mary unless your peers and the nuns said that you were a person of great worth, high leadership quality and all the rest of it. I went off on my own to do a one-day retreat and then on 8 December I was made a Child of Mary. It was a lovely ceremony with candles all around, and I wore a veil and a big blue ribbon with the Child of Mary medal on it. I was bursting with awareness of the importance of it all and always wore this big ribbon on my plump green chest.

But it was not to last. A very short time afterwards I was stripped of the medal, just like a soldier is cashiered from the army by having his buttons cut off. It happened like this. Most of the boarders had boyfriends. I didn't have any, but I became very popular by volunteering to post the boarders' letters to their boyfriends. I used to stuff the letters down the front of my gymslip and smuggle them out for posting. One evening, I was accosted by a nun, who kept talking to me and asking me if I was all right, because I looked as if I were dying of angina, clutching my chest. 'Oh, I'm fine, Mother, fine,' I blurted out, as one by one the letters slipped from under my gymslip. It was so humiliating as the nun picked up the letters address to Master Sean O'Brien, Master John Smith and so on. I really felt that the pit of hell was opening up in front of me.

'Isn't it very sad my dear,' she said icily, 'that you are not a person to be trusted? Tomorrow morning at assembly you will give your medal back.'

And so it was that, red-eyed, I handed back my Child of Mary medal. It was a bitter disappointment, particularly in the hot-house atmosphere that existed in a girls' school in those days. I did become a kind of heroine by refusing to disclose who had given me the letters, but if, like me, you were on the way to sainthood it wasn't enough being a popular heroine. I would have much preferred to have been a Child of Mary.

The Long March

On 28 August 1963, two hundred thousand people assembled for a 'March on Washington' in which they would call for civil rights for all US citizens and an end to racism. It was the start of a long and arduous campaign that would eventually bear fruit. The marches were inspired by a passionate address by MARTIN LUTHER KING, Jr. In the excerpt below, King outlines his dream for the future.

I say to you today, my friends, though, even though we face the difficulties of today and tomorrow, I still have a dream. It is a dream deeply rooted in the American dream. I have a dream that one day this nation will rise up, live out the true meaning of its creed: 'We hold these truths to be self-evident, that all men are created equal.'

I have a dream that one day on the red hills of Georgia sons of former slaves and the sons of former slave-owners will be able to sit down together at the table of brotherhood. I have a dream that one day even the state of Mississippi, a state sweltering with the heat of injustice, sweltering with the heat of oppression, will be transformed into an oasis of freedom and justice.

I have a dream that my four little children will one day live in a nation where they will not be judged by the colour of their skin but by the content of their character. I have a dream ... I have a dream that one day in Alabama, with its vicious racists, with its governor having his lips dripping with the words of interposition and nullification, one day right there in Alabama little black boys and black girls will be able to join hands with little white boys and white girls as sisters and brothers.

A Dream of Peace

It is said that a picture in a London shop window prompted WILLIAM BUTLER YEATS to write his dream-poem 'The Lake Isle of Innisfree'. It is a fantasy of escape from the city's bustle to a place where peace would come 'dropping slow'.

The Lake Isle of Innisfree

I will arise and go now, and go to Innisfree,
And a small cabin build there, of clay and wattles made:
Nine bean-rows will I have there, a hive for the honey-bee,
And live alone in the bee-loud glade.

And I shall have some peace there, for peace comes dropping slow,
Dropping from the veils of the morning to where the cricket sings;

There midnight's all a glimmer, and noon a purple glow,
And evening full of the linnet's wings.

I will arise and go now, for always night and day
I hear lake water lapping with low sounds by the shore;
While I stand on the roadway, or on the pavements grey,
I hear it in the deep heart's core.

The Birth of the Model T

Henry Ford, the son of an Irish emigrant to the USA, set up a car manufacturing plant in Co. Cork in 1916 which grew to become one of Ireland's most successful industries. Through a quirk of historical fate, accountant EUGENE CLARKE joined the Ford team and went on to become the first native managing director of a plant that employed over five thousand people.

I had studied commerce and accounting in London, but I became homesick and came home to find employment in Skerries Tuition College in Dublin. At Easter 1916 I went down to visit my girlfriend in Bantry and we had a lovely time cycling around West Cork, unaware of what was going on in Dublin. When I went to return I was told there were no trains running to Dublin as there was 'some serious trouble up there'. I was stranded in Cork but managed to get some temporary employment there, until I heard that Henry Ford was planning to open an automobile plant by the Lee. He had bought Cork racecourse – a site of one hundred and fifty acres with river frontage – for the purpose. I applied for a job and was fortunate that they needed an accountant to look after payroll, purchasing and so on. I was the second Irishman to be employed at the Cork plant.

From the Memoir of Henry Ford: *We chose Ireland for a plant because we wanted to start the country along the road to industry. There was some personal sentiment in it too. My ancestors came from near Cork and that city with its wonderful harbour has an abundance of fine industrial sites. Cork has for many years been a city of casual labour and extreme poverty. We started our plant there with three men from Detroit in charge of operations and now (1926) we have one thousand eight hundred men employed. Eight hours a day, five days a week at a minimum of two and three-pence an hour. Steady money – something few if any of the men had ever known before.*

Within days of my employment there were three hundred men on the payroll. For the first two years they were involved in the construction of the plant under the direction of Raymond Brown. Henry Ford had grown up on a farm and was a great agriculturalist as well as being an inventor and his constant ambition was 'to lift farm drudgery off flesh and blood and lay it on steel and motors'. He realised his ambition with the Fordson tractor. When food supplies became scarce during the Great War, Lloyd George appealed for help to Ford and he despatched five thousand Fordsons to England at a cost of £150 each.

From the Memoir of Henry Ford: *It was these tractors, run mostly by women, that ploughed up old estates and golf courses and let all England be planted, without taking away from fighting manpower or crippling forces in the munitions factories.*

After the war, the demand for tractors fell and the Cork plant concentrated on making engines and rear axles for cars. These were shipped to Manchester for assembly. The car in question was, of course, the famous Model T.

From the Memoir of Henry Ford: *I will build a motor car for the great multitude. It will be large enough for the family, but small enough for the individual to run and care for – and so low in price that no man making a good salary will be unable to own one and enjoy, with his family, the blessings of hours of pleasure in God's great open spaces …*

My involvement with Ford's was a pure quirk of fate – stranded in Cork because of a rebellion in Dublin. In fact, I still have that return ticket from Cork!

An Appeal

*In September 1984, I was a radio producer with RTÉ.
I wrote the following letter to the editor of* Access, *the
RTÉ in-house newspaper.*

———

Sir,

I have just returned from a most relaxing and
enjoyable family holiday. Nothing fancy. A little
chalet on the sun-drenched Costa del Rosslare,
daily swims, picnics and football on the beach, a
bit of tennis when the weather wasn't too hot, a
couple of meals in Kelly's Hotel, but most of all
unwinding and enjoying the lazy hazy days of
summer.

The only thing that 'spoiled' the holiday were
those haunting pictures in television documentaries
and news features of the famine in Africa. The sheer
scale of the suffering, particularly the suffering
of the children, arouses a mixture of emotions:

anger that the world's riches should be so unfairly divided; sorrow that my fellow man should suffer so; frustration – what can I do to help? And quite frankly fear that in the next world we who enjoyed more than a fair share of the world's 'riches' will have an awful lot to answer for …

I have no intention of quoting scripture. I am not a do-gooder. I am not interested in political arguments about the Third World. I am not trying to salve my conscience. I simply want to *do something now* to help those suffering people of Africa. So, there are appeals, bank-giros, sponsorships – various ways of helping. Personally, I find it usually difficult or inopportune to fork out ten or twenty pounds at one go (probably selfishness on my part). But why not a painless deduction of say 'a pound a pay cheque' into a fund for famine relief? Just think – if every employee in RTÉ agreed to this it would mean a fund of over £50,000 per annum …

I know there are many deductions eroding our pay cheques already but surely we could make this one little sacrifice (the equivalent of soup and a roll once a fortnight) for such a worthy cause. Who will join me in the 'Pound a Pay Cheque' Campaign? Please ring me at Extension 2660 or drop me a note to the Education Department, Radio Centre. And please do it now.

Yours sincerely,
John Quinn

I am glad to report that my colleagues answered the call and within six months the RTÉ Staff One World Fund was established. (One of many such funds established by various organisations at that time.) Thirty-five years later, the fund continues to flourish. The 2019 AGM noted that the fund had 395 members, who contributed €53,600 in 2018. It had funded thirteen projects in 2017, ranging through water hygiene, basic education, agriculture, healthcare and micro enterprises. Over the thirty-five years the fund would have contributed €1.5 million.

It delights me to know this – but this is no exercise in vainglory. The dedicated work of committee members and the generosity of the RTÉ staff are the story. Every venture begins with a small step. In my case, it meant only taking a few minutes to write a letter.

A Knock at the Door

Sometimes, what turns out to be an extraordinary venture begins in the simplest way, such as a knock at the door. In this case the door was ours and my late wife OLIVE QUINN answered it.

———

Sometime late in 1982, Claire Dunphy knocked on our door. Claire was the local public health nurse and she lived just around the corner from us in Greystones. She knocked on the door with a purpose.

In her daily work, Claire was coming across an increasing number of physically disabled adults who were literally prisoners in their own homes. They had no social outlets, no opportunities to develop their talents, to be the people they could be. This wasn't right, Claire thought. To compound matters, the disabled were being cared for day in, day out – and night in, night out – by devoted partners, parents or family members who, in many instances, had given up their careers to care for the loved ones. Equally, the carers were very often prisoners – willing prisoners, but prisoners nonetheless. This certainly wasn't right, Claire thought. The system was failing these people. She voiced her opinions but nobody was listening. 'We need someone who is *political*, someone who will kick up a fuss,' she said to a friend. 'I'll try Olive Quinn!' She obviously knew Olive Quinn better than most, and when Olive opened the door to Claire that day, it was a symbolic beginning to a quite extraordinary adventure.

As a child and a young woman, Olive was always teased by her family as being the 'Patron of Lost Causes'. If there was a 'lame duck' or a down-and-out in the vicinity, Olive would be the one who would show practical concern for that person – 'Oh, another of Olive's lost causes,' they would say. Scoff they might – and we all occasionally scoffed – but Olive had a fierce sense of justice. She simply could not understand, and would not tolerate, injustice in any form and refused to walk away from it. Of course, we could be embarrassed by all of this. 'Look, don't get involved,' we would say. 'Not our business. The government's fault. Leave it. You'll get yourself into a mess. And what about your own health?' All the excuses we could muster for our own inadequacy, our guilt. They cut no ice with Olive, and only made her more determined. Once she got her teeth into injustice, she was the proverbial terrier. Would not let go. Oh, she was 'political' all right. Claire Dunphy had chosen well. The test case that Claire outlined that day concerned Helen Clarke. Helen was the only child of Kevin and Phyl Clarke and, at the age of twenty-one, with a wonderful life before her, she developed a brain tumour that paralysed her and left her with a life of quiet desperation in a wheelchair. Kevin, a recovering alcoholic, had to continue working to maintain his family. Phyl was frail and arthritic. A desperate situation. Olive went to visit them and the Clarke family subsequently became good friends of ours.

Olive was convinced about Claire's argument. There were other Helen Clarkes about. A centre was needed to provide care and development on a daily basis, and equally, to give respite to carers. And so, the struggle began.

The initial response from the health board was disappointingly predictable. The numbers weren't there to justify a day centre. 'A handful of people,' they said. Olive joined forces with a friend, Mary Hackett, and with Pádraigín Hughes, whose husband was disabled. They did their own research, carried out their own census, travelling the highways and byways of North Wicklow. The 'handful of people' grew to thirty, forty, maybe more. The three women made their case and continued to lobby. They enlisted the support of Monsignor John O'Connell, the dynamic parish priest of Holy Redeemer Parish in Bray, a parish noted for its range of innovative social services. He, in turn, enlisted the help of prominent businessmen in the town who would act as trustees for the project. The wheels were turning.

Olive was in her element now. The politician in her revelled in a challenge. This was not charitable work, in her view. It was simply a matter of rights, of justice. The physically disabled and their carers had been 'lost causes', but their patron had arrived, and woe betide the authorities who took her on! The project needed a name. Olive came up with one: Open Door. A symbol of inclusiveness, of welcome. The disabled would not be 'patients' or 'clients'. They would be *members* of a warm, embracing community. Olive threw her energy and time totally and willingly into Open Door. Her energy was limited, given her health problems, but it was never a disadvantage. She had the time. The children were all at school and, while they now recall Mum being almost constantly on the telephone (we won't talk about the phone bills) when they came home from school, they were always her first concern. And the husband? Well, he was good at writing letters. So he wrote letters (willingly) to ministers, health board personnel, the Wheelchair Association. He wrote letters.

It all came to fruition in December 1984, when agreement was reached and the Open Door Day Centre for the Physically Disabled opened in temporary premises in Fatima House, a Legion of Mary hall in Bray. The beginnings were rudimentary

– six members and a staff of three. The members were collected by ambulance and brought to a place where they could socialise, pursue interests and crafts, avail of physiotherapy and occupational therapy, and have a hot meal delivered daily from Loughlinstown Hospital. But from day one, what immediately impressed the visitor was the wonderful atmosphere of warmth, enjoyment and love that permeated the centre. I was so happy for the three women who had worked so hard, but I was immeasurably proud of Olive. She had proved that it *ought* to be done, it *could* be done – and now it *was* done. And Claire Dunphy had a knowing smile on her face …

Today, thirty-five years later, the Open Door Day Centre thrives in a new purpose-built premises on Vevay Road, Bray with some eighty members and an expanded range of services. And I am prouder than ever of the woman who opened the door to Claire Dunphy in 1982.

The Beginning of

A CAREER

———

'I recognised the immense
reach of having an idea.'

GETTING A START

The first winner of the Pushkin Prize was JOHNNY McDAID, now a multi-instrumentalist with the world-renowned group Snow Patrol.

———

My favourite word is 'start'. I love it as a noun, as a verb, as an instruction and as an idea.

Everything has a start. This sentence, that thought, everyone you have ever known, everything you have ever seen or imagined began somewhere. Every poem you've ever read, everything you have ever heard and every theory, discovery, notion or creation has had a start.

All of the things we know about began somewhere, and all of them have something in common. They had a place in which to begin. They had, for better or for worse, a start.

In 1987, I met Sacha Abercorn. She came to St Brigid's Primary School in Derry, where I was making a start as a very average school show singer and as one of the worst football players ever to come from anywhere. I was okay at music and I loved writing so I was intrigued by Sacha and her Pushkin Prize, a creative writing organisation she had set up to encourage creativity amongst the children of Ireland.

The Pushkin experience became part of my DNA and it never left me. I was still made of the same molecules, I was still the same person, but I was altered by it and shown a path to a world where the creative spirit could thrive. No longer did my poetry live alone on shreds of torn jotters flung around my bedroom, no longer did the stories I wrote fall away into some fanciful waste of time. Through Pushkin, people read my words and they were given meaning on the outside. It was the first time I recognised the immense reach of having an idea.

The Pushkin Trust has come a long way in a quarter of a century. It has grown into a beautiful collective of creative, inspired people, all of whom strive to help realise Sacha's vision of what might be if we just wondered out loud. It has guided and nurtured some of the most talented minds to come from our little bit of land, North and South, and it has shown us that there is a way to freedom, and to a realisation of the self through an exploration and expression of the human psyche.

Pushkin showed me a place where anything can be, where anything is possible and where we are what we want to be. That place is close to every single one of us. It is in us and like everything that is, it just needs a beginning.

In Pushkin, I was given a start and I have not stopped since.

Two Views

When you are starting out as a writer, approval is everything, while rejection can be damning. JOHN B. KEANE knew both sides of the story.

———

I had two teachers in secondary school. One disapproved altogether of my attempt at creative writing and one day kicked me with his boot on the posterior, struck me with his fist on the head and slapped my face with his open palm till I was dizzy, all because I dared to quote one of my own poems during an elocution class. It was a poem about the street where I was born and the people who lived in it then. Compensation was to come.

The other was a Greek teacher and during his classes I took to writing sonnets or what I believed were sonnets. One day he lifted my exercise book and surveyed the partly finished sonnet. 'I like it,' he said. 'Keep at it and you'll write a good poem sooner or later.'

The first teacher prophesied that I would be a waster. The second prophesied that I would be a writer. The moral: take abuse in your stride and the praise will come.

The Student

It is 21 March 1960. I am a trainee primary teacher in St Patrick's College, Drumcondra, Dublin. The week I have dreaded has arrived: teaching practice. I must stand before a class of forty raucous ten-year-old boys in the Model School attached to the college – and teach for the first time. The class teacher, Stan O'Brien, will sit at the bottom of the classroom and write observation notes on the student teacher's performance. I am earnest, eager, committed – and terrified. Many years later, after Stan's death, someone came across his observation notes and sent them to me.

———

Seán Ó Cuinn. Junior Student. 21-3-60.

Manner: Ponderous and austere. Voice strong, clear articulation and emphatic enunciation.

Well-built, good appearance, excellent deportment.

Method and Preparation: Layout and research seem good but are adversely affected by 'manner'. In general, the mechanics of teaching are appreciated and understood, but not always applied. His questions do not always encompass the class and the matter is often handled indecisively. Irish is not secure at times, needs attention.

Discipline: Not firm enough.

General: Exceedingly earnest in his approach, diligent in preparation, but his stern and stilted attitude precluded contact with the children and no amount of conscientiousness can overcome this lack. He must 'loosen up', present a less funereal countenance to the children and inject some humour into his teaching. (There was one faint ray, when the children said, 'That was the first time the student smiled!') All in all, he is a solid man who will, I am sure, make an efficient if not an inspiring teacher.

———

My observations after almost sixty years: Fair comment, Stan. I was terrified, but in the words of Lao Tzu, 'A journey of a thousand miles begins with a single step.' And my wife made hay with that 'funereal countenance' remark for years!

Decision Time

*With the end of secondary schooling comes the beginning
of a career. Choices have to be made. JENNIFER
JOHNSTON came from a background of theatre (her
mother, Shelah Richards, was a stage director) and
writing (her father, Denis Johnston, was a journalist
and writer). Which way would Jennifer go?*

———

When I left school at seventeen years of age I did
say that I wanted to go on stage but my parents were
distinctly unenthusiastic about the idea. At one point
my father said to me, in a very patronising way, 'Oh,
you just want to be an *actress*,' and I thought there
must be something terribly wrong about that. My
mother's reaction was, 'Well you can either go to
Trinity College or I will see if Hilton (Edwards) will
give you a job.' I was living at home and I presumed
that they both wanted me to go to Trinity College.
It wasn't really an either-or situation. I didn't fight
my corner at all. I went to Trinity College.

The Beginning of a Career / 107

I have no regrets at all now about that decision. I feel that if I had gone into the theatre I wouldn't have done any writing; and I think that I am a much better writer than I would ever have been an actress. I would have liked to direct plays, but at that point in my life directing was a distant dream which would have been totally unattainable. I am very glad that I went to college – and that in itself was not easy. I had never really settled down to work at school and at the age of seventeen I suddenly realised that I did not even have a basic education. I had great difficulty getting into Trinity and when I did get in, I was terribly disillusioned with what was on offer – just sitting in a class of an enormous size, listening to tiresome old men talking to us about Shakespeare. I had expected to be illuminated by university because I had a vision of all those lovely intelligent people, growing up acquiring knowledge and knowing what to do with it, but university wasn't like that at all. It was a peculiar time in university because it was just after the war and there was a great influx of ex-service men. You couldn't really call them men, God love them. They were senior to the ordinary students, mostly in their early twenties. They were both glamorous and dangerous. They had all been at war and had seen something outside Ireland, which none of the rest of us had done. They seemed terribly sophisticated, but most of the time they were getting drunk and making an awful nuisance of themselves. They were frightening to us, which in a way made us seem very much younger than in fact we were. We felt like schoolchildren because we had to fight against this great body of 'sophistication'.

All the World's his Stage

It took a childhood friend to remind CYRIL CUSACK that from his schooldays he had a singular ambition.

———

I was walking thoughtfully along the Grand Parade by the canal in Dublin when suddenly Grace appeared, and Grace, a buxom, mature lady with a quiet face, said, 'Of course, you won't remember me, but we were in the same class together at St Paul's in Bray.'

Good heavens – and that was over fifty years ago!

'And do you remember,' she continued, 'one morning Mr Moore, the headmaster, picking us out with his wooden pointer, one by one, and asking us what we were going to be?'

I puzzled my brain.

'And when he pointed at you he said, "And you now, you – what are you going to be?" You answered … do you remember?'

A flock of memories came pelting through my mind. Part of Sylvester's Pantomime Company, we had arrived in Bray where we were to play at the Pavilion, a faded hall sprouting little minarets somewhat limply after the grand manner of the pavilion at Brighton. There, for 'one week only', a different pantomime was performed every night. As a child actor I appeared in three of these – a babe in *Babes in the Wood*, the hind part of the pantomime horse in *Ali Baba and the Forty Thieves*, and the cat in *Dick Whittington*.

Her initial question still unanswered, Grace was listening.

'Yes,' I went on, 'and there was that night when the tail of the cat got caught in the painted roller curtain and I was swung up dangling over the footlights. Jim Johnson, the comedian, rushed over to disentangle me but not before the Bray audience had had their biggest laugh of the evening.'

Grace was persistent. 'Do you not remember? What you said to Mr Moore when he asked you that?'

'No,' said I.

'Ah, go on!'
'No, what did I say?'
'You answered … I'm going to be a great actor.'

A Commentator – or Something

It was evident from a very young age that the late great JIMMY MAGEE would realise his childhood dream and become a passionate sports reporter.

'If Jimmy doesn't become a footballer or runner, he'll end up being a commentator or something.' That's what our neighbour Willie Lowe said to my father in those far off days at the end of the last war.

Willie Lowe had been observing my antics and listening to my voice pieces long before I realised that anyone was aware of my dream factory.

Since the age of seven or eight I'd been doing commentaries on imaginary matches. Most of the time I played in the games myself. I recall being part of the Cavan forward line of 1947 – the Polo Grounds team: Tony Tighe, Mick Higgins, Columba McDyer, Joe Stafford, Peter Donohoe and Jimmy Magee. You'll agree it was quite an achievement to play in *and* commentate upon the same game. Then each weekend I presented a half-hour programme of reports and interviews. I acted as compère and under different names I delivered all the reports and acted as both interviewer and interviewee. What I do on Sundays now on RTÉ Radio is merely an extension of those makey-up days of innocent childhood.

Willie Lowe was also an inspiration in another area, that of competition. He had me on the brink of the four-minute mile long before Roger Bannister was heard tell of ... I was within one hundredth of a second of becoming history's first sprinter under ten seconds. I didn't know it then, but men like Willie Lowe are the stuff of which coaches are made.

A good coach is the one who can cajole the best out of a person; he's the one the aspiring athlete wants to please on each performance; he's the person who never allows you reach the limit, yet always makes you believe that you are almost there.

'Your Jimmy will end up being in sport,' he told my father, and even though my father was ailing from terminal illness at the time, I knew somehow that he believed it. Perhaps today the two of them are tuned in whenever I get paid for doing what I've wanted to do since I was in second class at school – 'be a commentator or something'.

God Bless the Nuns

SPIKE (TERENCE) MILLIGAN grew up in India where his father was a soldier. According to him, it was the nuns who started him on his zany comedic career.

My mother was inclined to cosset me as a child so she sent me to a convent school – the Convent of Jesus and Mary in Poona, India – when I was five. I did very well there – came first in my class regularly, under the tutelage of Mother Fabian, a tall red-faced nun bursting with repression!

The nuns were responsible for putting me on the stage. They hadn't quite worked out how to change the scenery quickly between the acts, so they dressed me up as a clown and I had to go out in front of the curtains and generally jump up and down until the nuns were ready and they would whisper 'That's all, Terry! That's all!' Then I would disappear and the second act began. I suppose I haven't stopped clowning since!

SMILE!

Businessman FEARGAL QUINN, founder of the Superquinn chain of supermarkets, discovered at an early age the importance of a smile.

Somebody said to me last week that they were surprised at how much influence my teenage years had had on me. I think most young people don't know how important those teenage years are. Almost every day, they are learning things that will be important later in life. It isn't necessarily just the academic end of things, but also the experiences that we have, the things that happen, that can play a very large part in our lives.

By far the greatest influence in my life was my father. I grew up in a holiday camp. That was his business. Since guests who came to Red Island in Skerries paid for everything on the day they arrived, there was nothing we could do to take money off them; we couldn't sell them anything extra. So my father's one objective was to get them to come back again. That's what I call in my book *Crowning the Customer*, the 'boomerang principle' – 'Can we get the customer to come back again?'

When I went into business in my first shop in Dundalk, I was strongly influenced by this objective that I had obviously inherited from the years spent working side by side with my father, but I discovered that my competitors weren't driven by the same objective. Theirs was to see how much they could make from the customer on that visit. Our view was that that was only secondary to getting the customer to come back again.

The holiday camp on Red Island was a great way to grow up. It was a business which covered so many different areas. I worked in the kitchen, I worked as a lounge boy, I worked in the office, I worked almost everywhere. One of the better years I had was working as a photographer. I discovered very early on that the photographs that sold best were those of people smiling. Therefore, one of the photographer's jobs was to get people to laugh. I discovered that I actually enjoyed getting people to laugh, even if I had to use the same routine over and over again, because, like a comedian, it was a different audience each time.

There's an old story about a company, I think it was IBM which, when they were taking on a salesman, only interviewed people who had a white handkerchief in their breast pocket because if you didn't wear a white handkerchief in your breast pocket you were unlikely to fit in as an IBM man. Our white pocket test is the ability to smile. So, when we hold interviews at Superquinn, somebody may be very good at giving change and very good at knowing the prices and at filling shelves, but if they are not able to smile, they probably aren't suitable to be a Superquinn employee. That may seem very tough, but it's better to find out from the beginning rather than be a square peg in a round hole.

Two Wheels

As travel writer, DERVLA MURPHY has explored some of the most exotic and inaccessible parts of the world on her bicycle. A childhood birthday present started her on that path.

———

For my tenth birthday I was given a present of a second-hand bicycle by my parents and an atlas by Pappa – which I suppose was an ominous sign, considering that I would spend so much of my life exploring the world on a bicycle. I recall on one of my cycling trips as a child resolving to cycle to India one day. Having consulted the atlas I discovered that there was almost no water between Ireland and India, so it would be India for me. There was no more convoluted reason than that for the original decision. But having made that decision I became very interested in India, and during my adolescence I read a lot about that country and I acquired an Indian penfriend, a Sikh girl called Mahn Kaur, with whom I corresponded for five years. Mahn Kaur's letters kindled an even greater interest in India – its people, its history and its various religions.

I loved cycling. I loved the freedom it brought and I loved exploring the beautiful countryside around Lismore. Cycling was not without its trauma, however. I set off one December morning to cycle to the top of Knockmealdown mountain, but the journey took longer than I had imagined, and on my way down a cloud came down on the mountain and I went totally astray. I spent the night in an old animal shelter and was found by a farmer the next morning. When I was eventually brought home, I was quite ill and spent the next fortnight in bed. However, that experience didn't deter me. A year or so later, I cycled all the way to Helvick Head and back – a journey of fifty miles – in one day.

Ink in his Veins

Author of a number of books about the lore and language of his native Dublin, ÉAMONN Mac THOMÁIS reckons that from his schooldays the ink was in his veins – almost literally.

What other kid do you know of in Ireland who tried to poison the whole class? All fifty-four of them. You see, the Master was out having a smoke and we were left to our own devices. Oh, 'devices' is right – without the 'de'! Anyway, after we cogged the coming 'ecker' so that, like the Boy Scouts, we'd be prepared, the class looked to me for leadership and entertainment. Éamonn, which was pronounced 'Yammon', was called out by every boy. What will we do, Yammon? Show us a trick, Yammon? Any jokes, Yammon?

What could I do, only go into the breach and give leadership. 'Right,' said I, 'here goes. Do you all see me steeler? (My big steel marble.) Well I'll give my steeler to the boy who drinks the most ink. But everyone must give me something as an entrance fee.'

Before you could say 'Jack Robinson', I was loaded with goodies. Chestnuts, cigarette pictures, bullseyes, Peggy's legs, even ha'pennies, they were all wanting a go to own the big steeler. Little did they know that I was going to be the best drinker in the class. You see, I had a lot of training. Every time the Master wanted new ink he sent me to the yard water-tap with a bag of brown ink powder and a large ink bottle. One day I tried a mouthful, just to see what it tasted like; it wasn't bad. It was a long way from ginger beer but still it wasn't bad.

Did you ever see fifty-four boys with blue lips ... blue tongues ... blue faces ... blue eyes and blue hands? Well none of them even took quarter as much as me, but the roars and screams brought the Master in like a flash. 'Janey Mac, I'm poisoned!' they were all shouting.

Leadership in Ireland was betrayed again and the Master confiscated all me goodies and the big steeler to boot. Six biffs on each hand every time the clock struck while the rest of the class prayed to save them from the poison ink. I could see myself in Mountjoy Jail and hear the judge roaring at me for killing fifty-four schoolboys.

No one died. No one even got sick. They all laughed at me and me steeler. But do you know what? All that ink I drank as a chiseller went into my veins and I have to keep writing every day to try and get rid of it.

The Colonel's Stamp

When PETER USTINOV joined the army during World War II, he learned a very important lesson on day one.

———

When we first went into the army, we had to report to Canterbury and I sat there miserably with my kit-bag, in my civilian clothes, in front of a fire. Nobody had yet decided what to do with us and there was an old soldier – an old sweat, a regular – sitting in front of the fire too, casting his mind back to his own first day. He said, 'I see you're going into the army. I find it difficult to remember the time when I first went in. I'm a volunteer, you see, a peace-time soldier, and I never moved up from private. I like it like that. But there was a story I heard when I first went in which might help explain the army to you.

'There were two soldiers, you see, on latrine duty. It was autumn and one was sweeping up and a sudden gust of wind caught up a piece of used toilet paper. Like an autumn leaf it floated in the air. They couldn't reach it and – before they could prevent it – it floated in through the Colonel's window. Now what were they to do? One of them said, "Look you go on working here. If anybody asks where I am, I've been taken short, right? And meanwhile I'll go up and see if the old man's in and try and recuperate that piece of paper." So, the man went off and came back five minutes later and the first one, who was still sweeping, said, "Did you get it?" And the other one said, "No, I was too late. He'd already signed it.'"

Finding Characters

An only child, MARY LAVIN spent her early childhood in Massachusetts, USA. Her Irish-born mother was homesick there and brought nine-year-old Mary home to Galway for 'a visit'. That first visit did much to nurture the young writer.

My mother eventually got her way about 'visiting' and returned with me to her native place – Athenry, Co. Galway. I had a rather curious existence there. We were supposed to be going back to America in a month or two so I did not go to school there initially. But we actually spent eight months there and for the first six months I didn't go to school. I was having a solitary life again – solitary but not lonely. Instead of the trees and flowers of Massachusetts I now had the company of *people*, which was new to me.

Even in my own mother's home there were so many people. She was the eldest of twelve children and most of them were at home, so I had this large extended family. Then there was the family shop, which meant that I met a lot more people. Outside the home and the shop, I was a great wanderer. I would wander all over the town and of course, having come from America, I was a real *persona grata*. I was in everybody's house, having barmbrack and cake and lemonade. They were probably asking me a lot of questions about my family, questions which I was only too ready to answer, but equally I was seeing the intimate side of their lives – all the rows, the love affairs, the jealousies and whatever. I was taking in all this, although I didn't realise it at the time. Later, when I began to write, this period in Athenry was to influence me greatly. I had never intended to be a writer. I had written a book or two early on, including a school story when I was about fourteen. But it was really only for fun – I was a bit of a show-off at the time.

But later when I came to write a story about an aunt of mine in Athenry, all of a sudden I knew that I had a facile gift. I had always been very good at essays in school and I knew that I could write; but

I hadn't realised the power there is in writing and how much I could extract out of myself by writing. I realised how much there was that I didn't know I knew until I began to write, and when I began to write it came out in a kind of involuntary way. When I wrote I cast the characters in the mould of the people in Athenry. I used them as prototypes for people like them that I had met elsewhere.

The Beginning of

A NEW TIME

———

'Ne'er saw I, never felt, a calm so deep!'

The Cry of the Deer

This eighth-century poem is attributed to ST PATRICK and has been entitled 'St Patrick's Breastplate'. Legend has it that the High King sent his troops to ambush St Patrick and his followers as they made their way to Tara. When the troops attacked they found themselves confronting a herd of deer.

It acquired an added resonance for me when I attended a boarding school run by the Patrician Brothers. We began each day with Mass and prayers in the oratory, prayers such as 'Christ with me, Christ before me, Christ behind me …'

———

I arise today
Through the strength of heaven:

Light of sun,
Radiance of moon,
Splendour of fire,
Speed of lightning,
Swiftness of wind,
Depth of the sea,
Stability of earth
Firmness of rock.

I arise today
Through God's strength to pilot me:
God's might to uphold me,
God's wisdom to guide me,
God's eye to look before me,
God's ear to hear me,
God's word to speak to me
God's hand to guard me,
God's way to lie before me,
God's shield to protect me,
God's host to save me
From snares of devils,
From temptations of vices,
From everyone who shall wish me ill,

Afar and anear,
Alone and in a multitude.

Christ to shield me today
Against poison, against burning,
Against drowning, against wounding,
So that there may come to me abundance of
    reward.
Christ with me, Christ before me, Christ behind
    me,
Christ in me, Christ beneath me, Christ above
    me,
Christ on my right, Christ on my left,
Christ when I lie down, Christ when I sit down,
Christ when I arise,
Christ in the heart of every man who thinks of
    me,
Christ in the mouth of every one who speaks of
    me,
Christ in every eye that sees me,
Christ in every ear that hears me.

I arise today

Through a mighty strength, the invocation of the
    Trinity,
Through belief in the Threeness,
Through confession of the oneness
Of the Creator of Creation.

Resolution

The month of February gives a lift to the heart. Winter darkness is starting to recede. There is a 'stretch in the evenings'. Nature is beginning to reawaken. For the blind poet ANTHONY RAFTERY, who spent his days wandering the roads of Connacht, the feast of St Brigid (1 February) brought new resolution and the anticipation of happier days when he would return to his beloved Co. Mayo. He captured those feelings in his poem 'Cill Aodáin'.

———

Anois teacht an Earraigh, beidh an lá dul chun síneadh
'S taréis na féil' Bríde, ardóidh mé mo sheol
Ó chuir mé i mo cheann é, ní stopfaidh mé choíche
Go seasfaidh mé síos i lár Chontae Mhaigh Eo.

———

A modern poet, MICHAEL COADY, offers this translation of RAFTERY'S poem of longing, 'The Blind Poet's Vision of Spring'.

The Blind Poet's Vision of Spring
from the Irish of Anthony Raftery (c.1784–1835)

With the coming of spring the light will be gaining,
so after Bríd's feast day I'll set my course —
since it entered my head I'll never rest easy
till I'm landed again in the heart of Mayo.
I'll spend my first night in the town of Claremorris
and in Bal' I'll raise my glass in a toast,
to Kiltimagh then, I could linger a month there
within easy reach of Ballinamore.

I testify here that the heart in me rises
like a fresh breeze lifting fog from the slopes
when I think on Carra and Gallen below it,
on *Sceathach a' Mhíle* or the plains of Mayo.
Killedan's a place where all good things flourish,
blackberries, raspberries, treats by the score,
were I to stand there again with my people
age would fall from me and I'd be restored.

New Year

*PATRICK KAVANAGH looks forward to
1943 with particular resolution in this untitled
poem.*

The New Year's unwritten page we view
As a lea field to plough and sow;
The memory of the weeds from the last-turned
    page comes through,
But only matters what this year we grow.
(31 December 1942)

The City Awakes

Dawn breaks over a slumbering city. There is peace. There is calm. A scene of pristine beauty captured by WILLIAM WORDSWORTH.

Composed upon Westminster Bridge, September 3, 1802

Earth has not anything to show more fair:
Dull would he be of soul who could pass by
A sight so touching in its majesty:
This City now doth, like a garment, wear
The beauty of the morning: silent, bare,
Ships, towers, domes, theatres, and temples lie
Open unto the fields, and to the sky;
All bright and glittering in the smokeless air.
Never did sun more beautifully steep
In his first splendour valley, rock, or hill;
Ne'er saw I, never felt, a calm so deep!
The river glideth at his own sweet will:

Dear God! The very houses seem asleep;
And all that mighty heart is lying still!

Summer is Icumen In

Just as the wandering poet Anthony Raftery welcomed February as the harbinger of spring, so does the Meath 'poet of the blackbird' FRANCIS LEDWIDGE hail the month of June as it marks the advent of the warm, colourful days of summer.

June

Broom out the floor now, lay the fender by,
And plant this bee-sucked bough of woodbine
    there,
And let the window down. The butterfly
Floats in upon the sunbeam, and the fair
Tanned face of June, the nomad gypsy, laughs
Above her widespread wares, the while she tells
The farmers' fortunes in the fields, and quaffs
The water from the spider-peopled well.
The hedges are all drowned in green grass seas,
And bobbing poppies flare like Elmo's light,

While siren-like the pollen-stained bees
Drone in the clover depths. And up the height
The cuckoo's voice is hoarse and broke with joy.
And on the lowland crops the crows make raid,
Nor fear the clappers of the farmer's boy,
Who sleeps, like drunken Noah, in the shade.

And loop this red rose in that hazel ring
That snares your little ear, for June is short
And we must joy in it and dance and sing,
And from her bounty draw her rosy worth.
Ay! Soon the swallows will be flying south,
The wind wheel north to gather in the snow,
Even the roses spilt on youth's red mouth
Will soon blow down the road all roses go.

Growing Old Disgracefully

For JENNY JOSEPH, the coming of old age would mean the start of a revolution. She would live life her way, break all the conventions of being a 'senior citizen', no matter how much it shocked people. And for a start, she would wear purple. You have been warned!

Warning

When I am an old woman I shall wear purple
With a red hat which doesn't go, and doesn't suit
    me,
And I shall spend my pension on brandy and
    summer gloves
And satin sandals, and say we've no money for
    butter.
I shall sit down on the pavement when I'm tired
And gobble up samples in shops and press alarm
    bells
And run my stick along the public railings

And make up for the sobriety of my youth.
I shall go out in my slippers in the rain
And pick flowers in other people's gardens
And learn to spit.

You can wear terrible shirts and grow more fat
And eat three pounds of sausages at a go
Or only bread and pickle for a week
And hoard pens and pencils and beermats and
    things in boxes.

But now we must have clothes that keep us dry
And pay our rent and not swear in the street
And set a good example for the children.
We must have friends to dinner and read the
    papers.

But maybe I ought to practise a little now?
So people who know me are not too shocked and
    surprised
When suddenly I am old, and start to wear
    purple.

The Beginning of a New Time / 145

The Beginning of
WISDOM

———

'The longest and most exciting
journey is the journey inward.'

UNCERTAINTY

One of the most compelling talks I have ever heard was given by WALTER MacGINITIE in his closing address to the World Reading Congress in Dublin in 1982. His theme was 'The Power of Uncertainty'. I was lucky to record it and I subsequently broadcast it on RTÉ Radio – several times. In fact, I could make a case for having it broadcast daily. The beginning of learning is uncertainty. The following is an edited version of the talk.

———

The power of uncertainty. An odd topic. What is it about? You must all have a guess or two, and together must have a great factory of guesses.

A great factory of ideas about the power of uncertainty. How many interesting ideas you must have! See what uncertainty has done? But if you already knew my words, you would not have generated those ideas.

In George Bernard Shaw's *Back to Methuselah*, the Serpent in the Garden of Eden tells Adam, 'I take my chance ... nothing is certain but uncertainty. If I bind the future, I bind my will. If I bind my will I strangle creation.'

Uncertainty is frightening but liberating. We link uncertainty with fear, but it is the foundation of hope.

We link certainty with security, but it is the womb of indifference and the precondition for despair.

We extol certainty as positive thinking and associate it with action, with getting things done. And indeed, it can be a source of action. It takes a very certain man to shoot a pope, assassinate a president, or to give the orders for bloody terrorism or torture. We may call these actions extremes or aberrations. But extremes are the natural product of certitude. If

I am absolutely certain I am right, then it will appear to me that I am justified in anything. Think what atrocities have been committed by people who were absolutely sure they were right. Have you not seen news photographs of mobs of people, faces contorted, fists raised, hating? The next edition may show the people of the opposing mob, faces contorted, fists raised, hating. Does it never occur to anyone in such a mob that had they only been born at another time, or in another place, or with a different colour, or to a different religion, they would be in a different mob – perhaps the opposing mob – face contorted, fist raised, hating … someone else?

Uncertainty does not mean indecisiveness. It permits a rational basis for decisions. Uncertainty does not mean lack of planning or lack of action. It means planning based on reasonable alternatives and action based on current evidence. Uncertainty does not mean lack of courage. It means having the courage to reject the pleasures of self-righteousness and the pressures to conform.

Another point of view is always possible, and certainty is orthogonal to truth. Ambrose Bierce defined being positive as being 'wrong at the top of one's voice'. Jonathan Swift wrote, 'Who can deny that all men are violent lovers of truth, when we see them so positive in their errors?' Certainty is often justified by slogans – words, as Dylan Thomas said, 'to twist the shapes of thoughts into the stony idiom of the brain'. Certainty becomes a prison for the spirit and a pillow for the mind …

[W]e can understand that the power of uncertainty permits the development of new ideas and the correction of past mistakes. We can find guidance in our hope that people exposed to many ideas will choose humane ones, and we can find strength in our understanding that it is better to be seeking truth than to think we have found it.

Out-of-School Education

When the future business magnate TONY O'REILLY went to the Jesuit school, Belvedere College, Dublin much, if not most, of his learning took place outside the classroom.

———

I was a keen rugby player, as well as being a keen tennis and cricket player. I played soccer also, so my life essentially revolved around sport. But the Jesuits had the notion of *moderatio in omnibus* – the all-rounder was prized by them – so we had very substantial musical training, through Gilbert and Sullivan operas; we had an excellent chess club, which I enjoyed; we had cycling clubs and camera clubs and of course the inevitable debating societies, plus the academic world. But the Jesuits didn't emphasise the academic and I would describe my academic career at Belvedere as quite average.

I suppose I showed some early signs of being an entrepreneur there. I ran a penny library, which taught me a little bit about inventory control, in that nobody ever returned the books! We had an initial spurt of prosperity, as people paid us a penny for the loan of the book, so it did teach me a hard lesson that the initial success of an enterprise doesn't confirm its longevity.

In Belvedere there was one particularly profound influence on my life, Reverend Father Tom O'Callaghan. He was a mathematician of distinction, a theologian of great merit and probably the best rugby coach that I ever experienced in my entire rugby career. He was a theoretician, a hard taskmaster, a lover of the game – although he had never played it himself – and, because I was on what is called the Junior Cup team from the age of twelve, I had his influence for virtually all of the final six years of my rugby career in Belvedere. That was an extraordinary experience, because it brought an intellectual dimension into the game that I think stood by all of us who experienced his training for the rest of our lives.

I have always felt that rugby football was the great tutor, because it is really a template for life.

If you don't train, you don't get your rewards. So there is risk-reward ratio established clearly in your mind at an early stage. If you don't participate collegially with the other boys on the team, you are isolated. One learns about winning with grace and, more importantly, losing with grace. I call to mind Rudyard Kipling's poem, 'If':

> If you can meet with Triumph and Disaster
> And treat those two impostors just the
>   same …
> Yours is the Earth and everything that's in
>   it,
> And – which is more – you'll be a Man, my
>   son!

My father had given me these lines and he reminded me of them before we went out on the field to play in the Leinster Schools Cup Final. We lost to Blackrock by an intercept in the very last moment, when it looked as if we were about to win. I went behind the line, they took the kick and converted the try. The intercept was achieved by a very brilliant Blackrock player, Tom Cleary, who, funnily enough, had done the same thing the previous year against Clongowes, but this was more mortal since it was against us. He scored the winning try, the full-time whistle went and the sky was a blizzard of blue-and-white Blackrock scarves. He was festooned with his teammates and I went over and waited until they disengaged. I shook hands with him. We had lost the cup. My mother had bought a new hat as she had for the previous nine years, but, yet again, she had no opportunity to present the cup. It was a moment of very acute sadness in my life.

About twenty-eight years later I was president of Heinz and we had a major technical problem which could have led to a product recall and could have cost the company thirty to thirty-five million dollars. It required the support of a company called Del Monte. I flew to California to meet the president of Del Monte, who luxuriated in the extraordinary name of Jim Schmuck. I went to see Mr Schmuck and said to him, 'I'm O'Reilly, president of the Heinz company. We wonder if you could help us in this.' He then related to me a story of how his parish priest in Santa Barbara was a man called Fr McCarthy who was a scholastic at Blackrock College in Dublin when, as Schmuck rather poetically put it, 'you were engaged in the Superbowl while a schoolboy. At the last moment, when you had lost the game you showed some grace under pressure by shaking hands with the opponent from the side which had won the game. He thought you were a pretty good guy and advised me so, and so the Del Monte company will vote with Heinz on this issue.' That was the famous thirty-five-million-dollar handshake!

Writer, linguistics expert and political activist NOAM CHOMSKY grew up in a Jewish family in Philadelphia, USA – the only Jewish family in a largely Irish and German Catholic neighbourhood that was fiercely anti-Semitic. To counter that there was the influence of an intellectually enriching extended family.

Many of them had never been to school, but they lived in an atmosphere of quite high culture and also working-class culture, which were not dissociated at that time. They were very active intellectually in every domain.

These were immigrants, usually first-generation immigrants, maybe some early second-generation, working-class, largely unemployed. A few had gone on to school, one or two had gotten through college and become teachers. Some had not gotten past fourth grade; they had grown up on the streets. They were very deeply involved in working-class politics of the day, which meant the Communist Party for some and anti-Communist left for others, every fringe of radical opinion that you could think of. Of course, in those days that political activity didn't just mean having political opinions, it meant a life; it meant everything from the picnics to the summer vacations to concerts to everything else. A large part of their life was what we would nowadays call high culture: there would be debates about Steckel's critique of Freud, discussions about *Ulysses* and Cubist art and the latest concert of the Budapest String Quartet, as well as what was wrong with Lenin's version of Marx and what that implied for politics of the day.

Much of the excitement of this environment was focused for me around one particular uncle who hadn't gotten through elementary school. He happened to be disabled and, as a result, he was able to get a news stand, which became a very lively intellectual centre in the late thirties; a lot of European émigrés clustered around it, many of them German PhDs or psychiatrists and so on.

I remember going to work on the news stand in the evening by the time I was twelve or thirteen and it was a very exhilarating experience. I didn't understand much of what was going on, but it was exciting. Nobody bought many newspapers, but there was a lot of discussion.

The University of Life

Writer and practitioner in self-sufficiency JOHN SEYMOUR was born in England but ultimately settled in Co. Wexford. He was largely self-educated but considered his time in Africa as his university, beginning with the management of a farm in a remote part of Namibia.

————

There I came across an old box of books with which my boss's father – who was of Scottish descent – had tried to educate himself. There was an enormous amount of English literature in this box, but the white ants had eaten bits out of nearly all the books. White ants like books, but they don't read them, they eat them. So I would be reading *Henry IV* and I would come to a gap and have to work out for myself what Shakespeare would have said there. I recommend that as an education device. I had to use my imagination because of the white ants! I read all of the Shakespeare, all of Shaw and Fielding. It was the first time I really knew there was such a thing as English literature and I really got a lot of enjoyment out of it.

I stayed in Namibia for about two and a half years. I was managing a Karakul sheep farm, a breed which comes from central Asia. Their wool makes fur coats for rich ladies. That was the chief industry of the place. I had to look after about four thousand sheep and two thousand head of beef cattle. I was stuck away in the bush with nothing but African people – I couldn't speak a word of their language and they couldn't speak a word of mine. I learned to speak Afrikaans, which was the lingua franca, but I never learned any African language because there were four different language groups on the farm and if I learned one language then I wouldn't be able to speak to the other three quarters.

I loved Africa. I moved from the farm and spent a year deep-sea fishing in the south Atlantic and line fishing off Cape Town. I spent six months copper mining – every young man in those days had to have his term down the mine, otherwise he couldn't hold his head up. Then I got a job inoculating native cattle in northern Rhodesia, which is now called Zambia. I travelled over a huge area of central Africa. There were no roads and no cars – you walked and you had porters to carry your gear. You lived by your rifle, on what you could kill. I learned a great deal there – how to look after myself and be more or less self-sufficient. I would call Africa my university.

You Are Your Material

When FRANK McCOURT escaped from the misery of his Limerick childhood he became a teacher in New York. In his book Teacher Man, *he describes his attempts to teach creative writing to a particularly challenging group of high-school students. This wonderful passage is recommended for all would-be writers.*

Listen. Are you listening? You're not listening. I am talking to those of you in this class who might be interested in writing.

Every moment of your life, you're writing. Even in your dreams you're writing. When you walk the halls in this school you meet various people and you write furiously in your head. There's the principal. You have to make a decision, a greeting decision. Will you nod? Will you smile? Will you say, Good morning, Mr Baumel? Or will you simply say, Hi? You see someone you dislike. Furious writing again in your head. Decision to be made. Turn your head away? Stare as you pass? Nod? Hiss a Hi? You see someone you like and you say, Hi, in a warm melting way, a Hi that conjures up splash of oars, soaring violins, eyes shining in the moonlight. There are so many ways of say Hi. Hiss it, trill it, bark it, sing it, bellow it, laugh it, cough it. A simple stroll in the hallway calls for paragraphs, sentences in your head, decisions galore ...

Dreaming, wishing, planning: it's all writing, but the difference between you and the man on the street is that you are looking at it, friends, getting it set in your head, realising the significance of the insignificant, getting it on paper. You might be in the throes of love or grief but you are ruthless in observation. You are your material. You are writers and one thing is certain: no matter what happens ... you'll never be bored again. Never. Nothing human is alien to you. Hold your applause and pass up your homework.

Mr McCourt, you're lucky. You had that miserable childhood so you have something to write about. What are we gonna write about? All we do is get born, go to school, go on vacation, go to college, fall in love or something, graduate and go into some kind of profession, get married, have the two point three kids you're always talking about, send the kids to school, get divorced like fifty percent of the population, get fat, get the first heart attack, retire, die.

Jonathan, that is the most miserable scenario of American life I've heard in a high school classroom. But you've supplied the ingredients for the great American novel. You've encapsulated the novels of Theodore Dreiser, Sinclair Lewis, F. Scott Fitzgerald.

They said I must be joking.

The Beginning of
HOPE

—

'Every beginning is a promise …
flowering the way to work.'

A Miracle in Croke Park

As a member of a powerful Kerry Gaelic Football team in the 1960s and 1970s, DONIE O'SULLIVAN was familiar with success and the euphoria of All-Ireland final day in Croke Park, Dublin. He won four All-Ireland medals with Kerry (captaining the team in 1970) and seven National League medals. Yet all those days in Croke Park paled in comparison with a National League final in 1990. It was long after his playing days. Kerry weren't even playing.

———

I was just a spectator, but I've a very special reason for remembering that day as my son, Eoin, was able to come with me to the game. It was his first day back at a football game for over a year. The previous May, Eoin had been diagnosed with leukaemia and was very, very ill. He went through a very extensive course of chemotherapy and barely survived on a few occasions. It was our first outing together for a long time. It was a beautiful sunny day at the end of April and it was like a rebirth. Spring was in the air and Eoin was back to health again.

It made me appreciate more the feelings of Patrick Kavanagh in his poem of celebration, 'Canal Bank Walk'. It is a poem of rebirth and renewal. I will never forget that day in Croke Park as long as memory remains. I had the miracle there beside me. A great day and a day to be thankful to God. Everything after that is a bonus. Any time I would have walked into Croke Park before that day, I'd have taken things for granted: 'This is my right, nothing is going to happen to me.' You don't dwell on those things. Certainly that put life in perspective and no comparison to All-Ireland or League finals, winning or losing. That day in Croke Park was the highlight.

Difference

JOHN HUME spent most of his adult life working for peace, understanding and civil rights in Northern Ireland. For him, the foundation stone for achieving those aims was the acceptance of difference.

———

Cast your mind back fifty years to the end of the Second World War. Thirty-five million people lay dead across this continent, for the second time in this century. For centuries, the peoples of Europe saw difference as a threat and slaughtered one another. Their answer to difference was to conquer those from whom they differed. Who could have forecast, fifty years ago, that representatives of the peoples of all those countries would be sitting in a European parliament, as part of a united Europe? And the Germans are still German, and the French are still French. Who could have forecast fifty years ago that we would have a united Europe today? It is the best example in the history of the world of conflict resolution. When you consider the awful bitterness between the European peoples, and the slaughter that it led to, and that now we're all together: how did they do it? That's a question that everybody in every area of conflict should ask. The answer, like all profundities in life, is simple: they decided that difference is not a threat; that difference is of the essence of humanity; that it's an accident of birth what you're born, and where you're born, and whether that accident of birth is colour, creed or nationality, it is not the choice of the person being born; it is the way we were born. So why should it ever be the source of hatred or conflict? There are not two human beings in the entire human race who are the same.

Difference is of the essence of humanity. Difference enriches humanity, and the diversity enriches humanity. The peoples of Europe decided to respect their differences and to recognise that the divisions of centuries couldn't be healed in a week or a fortnight. They built institutions which respected their differences, which permitted them to work their common ground together, which is economics – bread on your table and a roof over your head; the right to existence, which is the most fundamental right, plus the right to a decent life.

The Right Word

In a collection on beginnings one could hardly not include a poem called 'Begin'. This wonderfully encouraging poem deserves inclusion in its own right, but it took on an added meaning in an extraordinary moment on live television in 1997. On the Late Late Show, *the host Gay Byrne telephoned a woman who had entered a postal competition. Her mother took the call. She was 'waking' her daughter who had just died in a traffic accident … The normally unflappable Gay turned to one of his guests, BRENDAN KENNELLY, who in a moment of genius recited his own poem 'Begin'.*

Begin

Begin again to the summoning birds
to the sight of the light at the window,
begin to the roar of morning traffic
all along Pembroke Road.

Every beginning is a promise
born in light and dying in dark
determination and exaltation of springtime
flowering the way to work.
Begin to the pageant of queuing girls
the arrogant loneliness of swans in the canal
bridges linking the past and future
old friends passing though with us still.
Begin to the loneliness that cannot end
since it perhaps is what makes us begin,
begin to wonder at unknown faces
at crying birds in the sudden rain
at branches stark in the willing sunlight
at seagulls foraging for bread
at couples sharing a sunny secret
alone together while making good.
Though we live in a world that dreams of ending
that always seems about to give in
something that will not acknowledge conclusion
insists that we forever begin.

New Life – New Hope

In 1998 the Good Friday Agreement brought peace to Northern Ireland after thirty years of violence and killing. The peace talks that led to the agreement had been chaired by SENATOR GEORGE MITCHELL. There had been many dark days during the talks, when the prospects of peace were very much in doubt, but 'a transforming event' in the Senator's personal life gave him the hope to persevere.

I will confess to you that I often thought of leaving, and especially in the spring of 1997 when we had a lengthy break in the negotiations for elections held in the British Parliament, and then District and Local Councils in Northern Ireland. Things looked very difficult and the prospects were slim. I discussed with my wife and friends of mine the possibility of leaving, and that was much on my mind throughout that summer and early fall.

And then, on 16 October 1997, a transforming event occurred in my life: my wife gave birth to our son. Every parent here knows what that means. In my case, it involved more than personal feelings; it involved my role in Northern Ireland. On the day that my son was born, I telephoned my staff in Belfast and asked them to find out how many babies had been born in Northern Ireland on that day. There were sixty-one. And I became seized with the thought: what would life be like for my son had he been born in Northern Ireland? What would life be like for those sixty-one babies, had they been born Americans?

The aspirations of parents everywhere are the same: to have children who are healthy and happy, safe and secure who get a good education and a good start in life, who have the chance to go as high and as far as talent and willingness to work will take them.

A few days after my son's birth, in what was, for me, a very painful parting, I left home to return to Belfast, to resume chairing the negotiations, and on that flight, I resolved that I would not leave, no matter what. I committed myself to the end, and promised to redouble my efforts to bring the negotiations to a successful conclusion.

And when I returned to the negotiations the next day, the delegates were very kind and expressed their congratulations on the birth of my son, and I told them of my thoughts. I told them that I was committed to stay until the end, that I was prepared to redouble my efforts, and I asked them for the same commitment. And I reminded them of the high obligation that they had as the elected representatives of the people of Northern Ireland not to let this opportunity pass.

We were able to bring it to a successful conclusion, thanks to their courage and perseverance. After the agreement was reached on Good Friday [1998], we came together for one last time. It was very emotional. Everyone was exhausted. We had stayed in negotiating session for nearly forty consecutive hours. For most of the previous two weeks, everyone had gotten little sleep, and so some cried; there were tears of exhaustion, of relief, of joy. I told the delegates, in my parting words, that for me, the Good Friday Agreement was the realisation of a dream, a dream that had sustained me through three and a half of the most difficult years of my life.

A State Is Born

In 1998 economist KEN WHITAKER, one of the prime architects of Ireland's economic development and growth, looked back on the State's seventy-five years in existence. Born in 1916, he had grown up with the State. Here, he reflects on the fragile beginnings of the new state.

———

We were well served by those who bedded down the democratic institutions. They took no risks and this was necessary because there was great doubt about the viability of the State – a doubt that persisted until the 1950s. I say we have come of age now because we are able to maintain an increased population at a reasonably high standard; there is no longer any net emigration; we are an open society economically – quite competitive – and therefore we have an independence that will serve us very well for the future.

The first national loan for £10 million was floated in 1923 and it was taken up by the Irish people when the Irish banks refused to contribute a penny. This indicated the confidence of the people in themselves. That would be £330 million in today's money. It was real democracy, and remember, Ireland then was a predominantly rural society. In 1922 there was only one person employed in industry for every eleven employed on the land (and many of the latter were in a state of misery). Now there are three in industry for every one on the land ... We must keep remembering too that Ireland over those seventy-five years was not the world. External influences have been of great importance – changes in world production and trade. For example, the Great Depression of the 1930s hit us badly when we had an economic war here. Then new technology affected transport and communications. Trade has opened up. Protection has been abandoned. So the world has become both smaller and a more competitive place and much more independent.

Education has been the key to our success. In a mere ten years the numbers participating at third level have doubled. There is still a low representation of children from poorer families but there are moves afoot to correct that. Overall the average family is three to four times better off than it was in 1922. In our time too, there have been great improvements in health. The death rate has been halved. Life expectancy has gone up by fifteen years or so and infant mortality – which was 10 per cent in the 1920s – is down to less than a tenth of that today.

It was a time of great satisfaction, because most of us who were engaged in that emergence felt that we were the first privileged generation of the new Ireland. We had good jobs, a good education, and here was a chance to apply what we had learned for the benefit of the country, as we saw it. That was a source of great satisfaction. Indeed, I remember thinking, going back to Wordsworth, how apt it was when he said, 'Bliss was it in that dawn to be alive, but to be young was very heaven!'

The Beginning of
A JOURNEY

———

'And in the mist of tears I hid from him.'

A Life-changing Experience

Writer, broadcaster and social philosopher CHARLES HANDY has been a major influential commentator on such areas as the future of work and the nature of organisations over the past forty years. A graduate of Oxford, he had been a Shell Oil executive in the Far East, had studied at the Sloan Business School at Massachusetts Institute of Technology and returned to England to set up an American-type business school. He was, it seemed, at the top of his career ladder. And then his father, a Church of Ireland minister in Co. Kildare, died. It was an event that would profoundly influence Charles Handy's life direction.

I went to his funeral, back in Ireland, at the old church that he had served for forty years. The place was packed with people crying and saying, 'This man meant more to us than anything else.' I suddenly realised that he had lived a rather special life, and the things that I had run away from, even despised, were actually incredibly valuable. So, in a way to apologise to him, I resigned my professorship, which was a crazy thing to do. It was a guaranteed job to sixty-five, a comfortable life and long vacations. I resigned all that and went to run a small centre, which happened to be based behind St George's Chapel in Windsor Castle, which educated the new bishops and the up-and-coming clergy who might become bishops. In between running these courses, I also held rather high-level meetings of about twenty-five leaders of society, convened by Prince Philip, who was my boss ultimately, to talk about social justice in society, the changing nature of work, the changing distribution of incomes, and such things. So there I was, on a clergy salary, living in a rectory, helping people less fortunate than myself. My life had gone full circle.

I met six thousand people in four years. I sat at the feet of a hundred and ten theologians over that period. It was an amazing learning experience for me. I was bombarded with the ideas of very interesting people and it broadened my horizons enormously.

I had a five-year contract, but I always think that you should leave one year before it is expected. By this time, I was actually talking and writing about what I call 'the future of work' and basically saying that a lot of people would have to spend a lot of their lives living what I called a 'portfolio life' – by their wits, bits and pieces of work, self-employed if you like, with a range of clients and customers and a range of skills. And wouldn't it be a very good idea if I actually tried to do that!

People thought I was crazy. I was forty-nine by then and at the height of my career. People expected me to go off and head a business school or a university – and that would have been an ambitious thing to do. Instead, I resigned from everything and went back to my flat in Putney in south London and my cottage in East Anglia to write books and do a bit of teaching. I had a £5,000 contract with the London Business School to do occasional bits of teaching and that was going to be my sole income.

It was frightening actually, but also incredibly freeing, because up until then half of me was Charles Handy but half of me was professor of this or head of that. I had to look over my shoulder to make sure I was saying the right thing. Suddenly I was all Charles Handy. I could be myself. I could say what I liked. I could arrange my life totally differently.

AI 4872

How could I ever forget it – the registration number of the first car I remember? The Quinn family saloon – a black (what else?) Baby Ford, my father's pride and joy, lovingly waxed and polished and regularly serviced in Smith's Garage in Trim. My father had always loved cars. He had arrived from Limerick in the 1930s in a sporty Morris Cowley with his wife and their firstborn, Kathleen, to Ballivor, Co. Meath to take up his position as a garda sergeant.

As his family grew, he moved on to a 'roomier' Baby Ford. Cars were still scarce on our roads when I arrived, the last of four children, in 1941. (Was not one of our most exciting hobbies the collection of registration numbers from the cars that passed through our village, particularly those Fairyhouse-bound on Easter Monday?) AI 4872 was our gateway to the world. We were brought on summer excursions to my father's homeplace, a magical farm in the distant wee hills of Monaghan. Four siblings packed into the back seat, experiencing wonder and delight rather than discomfort. (Little wonder that my sister Mary tumbled out the back door onto a grass verge as we negotiated a bend in Broomfield, Co. Monaghan!) On scalding summer Sundays, we travelled to the seaside in Bettystown. Even a short trip to Trim on a Sunday evening promised the excitement of a visit to the Royal Cinema, tea in McGonigle's and the regulatory recitation of the Rosary on the way home.

And on 8 December AI 4872 brought us to the Promised Land of Dublin. We shared the added burden of slain turkeys that my mother had reared from chicks, stopped off to despatch them to Carton Brothers Poultry Store in Cabra before parking right outside Clery's Department Store on O'Connell Street. A visit to Santa, ogling in wonderment at toys, new clothes for Christmas, high tea in the restaurant before completing a magical day at the variety show in the Theatre Royal.

Oh, little black gleaming Baby Ford – what journeys of discovery and delight you afforded us. You were the bright galleon that gave us our first glimpses of a wondrous world that lay beyond our sleepy village. I salute you and cherish your memory, AI 4872.

Three Ages of Man

JOHN F. DEANE recalls three stages of learning – at primary school, in boarding school and as a secondary-school teacher.

———

Achill Island

Our two-roomed school steamed with learning;
on bent backs a rhododendron wand beat rhythm
to our sing-song lore; brothers of St Francis wore
soft brown habits and white knotted cincture;
in their monastery chapel terracotta statues
smiled down on polished floors. We learned of
    God,
of Abraham and Noah, of towns outside
our island, colours beyond our skies. Once,
on the rhododendron driveway after a night
errand to the monastery, a barn owl hooted, each
gap in bushes sprang cowled figures without face.

Mungret College

The big grey building was a world apart where tall
figures in black stood poised above us, holding,
Napoleon-like, dark pandy-bats inside soutanes.
God was different here, bound up with long
corridors, sharp bells and strange, coiled, subjects.
Corridors shortened as we grew; one end closed
on a world of awe and movement, where a child
climbed trees to the sway of the wind; the other
opened on a world of adult lore, fast with cold
calculations. Nights were dark and silent,
and nightmares hovered in the dormitories.

St Aidan's

A few teachers sit around among
desultory spurts of small-talk; notice-boards
are crammed with this year's disarray; vague
sounds come from the class-rooms, the kettle
begins to hiss a little; on the long table
are scattered colonies of copies, uncorrected,
coats here and there, briefcases; the sun,
half-hearted, comes from that whirling world
        outside.

The Beginning of a Journey / 193

Soon a bell will ring, doors will open, lives
will buzz and move a moment; figures will change
in the staff-room; one will sigh, go to sit
back by the wall, light up his pipe and dream
of years to come.

A Conversion

Born in New York in 1897, DOROTHY DAY was a
journalist and political activist who dedicated her life
to peace, service of the poor and opposition to nuclear
weapons. At a young age her family moved to Chicago,
where she became aware of social injustice.

I walked the streets at sunset gazing at the
clouds over Lincoln Park, recognising the world
as supremely beautiful, yet oppressed somehow
with a heavy and abiding sense of loneliness and
sadness. When what I read made me particularly
class-conscious, I used to turn from the park with
all its beauty and peacefulness and walk down
to North Avenue and over west through slum
districts, and watch the slatternly women and the
unkempt children and ponder over the poverty of
the homes as contrasted with the wealth along the
shore drive. I wanted even then to play my part. I
wanted to write such books that thousands upon

thousands of readers would be convinced of the injustice of things as they were.

———

Later in life, DOROTHY DAY converted to Catholicism and founded the Catholic Worker movement and newspaper. Her attraction to Catholicism was influenced by Francis Thompson's poem 'The Hound of Heaven'.

———

It was on these cold bitter evenings that I first heard 'The Hound of Heaven', in an atmosphere of drink and smoke. Gene [playwright Eugene O'Neill] could recite all of Francis Thompson's poem, and would sit there, black and dour, his head sunk as he intoned: 'And now my heart is as a broken fount, wherein tear droppings stagnate.'

The idea of this pursuit by 'The Hound of Heaven' fascinated me. The recurrence of it, the inevitableness of the outcome made me feel sooner or later I would have to pause in the mad rush of living and remember my first beginning and my last end.

THE HOUND OF HEAVEN

I fled him, down the nights and down the days,
I fled him, down in the arches of the years;
I fled him, down the labyrinthine ways
Of my own mind; and in the mist of tears
I hid from him.

Francis Thompson

Amazing Grace

As a young sailor, JOHN NEWTON was heavily involved in the lucrative slave trade between Africa and the United States. A near-death experience, when his ship almost sank in a violent storm off the Donegal coast, prompted the beginning of a conversion from the slave trade. He studied the Bible and religious literature and became an Anglican priest in 1764. Eventually he renounced slavery, writing trenchantly about it and supporting its abolition. Newton also won fame as a hymn writer and is best remembered for 'Amazing Grace', which encapsulates his own story.

Amazing Grace

Amazing grace! (how sweet the sound)
That saved a wretch like me
I once was lost but now am found
Was blind, but now I see.

'Twas grace that taught my heart to fear
And grace my fears relieved
How precious did that grace appear
The hour I first believed.

Thro' many dangers, toils and snares
I have already come
'Tis grace hath brought me thus far
And grace will lead me home.

The Lord has promised good to me
His word my hope secures
He will my shield and portion be
As long as life endures.

A Beginning with
BOOKS

———

'They gave me the determination
to leave my darkness behind.'

The Company of Books

Many writers attest to the importance of childhood reading in setting them on the writing path. POLLY DEVLIN is one of those writers, even if the books of her childhood were an unusual collection.

———

Books were my escape and my path into the future – along with the good luck of having my sisters and my parents. My sisters are women of such quality that even talking to them would always give you a new stance and a new outlook on life; but books were a completely new avenue to the future. I had two sources of books. Above my father's pub – an Edwardian building – there was a loft into which had been put the books that had been jettisoned from the main house. These were books that my mother might have censored or books that people had got tired of – things like *Ripley's Believe It or Not* and a vast store of Victoriana – books on etiquette and household matters. Lying up in that loft, you could hear the murmur of the men's voices below us as they drank their Guinness; and the local dogs would come up to the loft because it was warm. We would lie up there, reading authors like Mrs Humphrey Ward, caught in our time warp.

The other source of books was, as it were, archives from the future. These were yearbooks which were sent to my mother by her half-sister, who was headmistress of a private school run by the Marymount nuns outside Los Angeles. I had never seen anything like those books. They were great big, fat, glossy things, bound with a kind of vinyl material – it was like a growing material, like a mushroom in my hand. When I opened each book there was a 'year' of the school spread out for me. There were photographs of girls with make-up and blonde hair, girls dancing, skiing, film-making, riding, making music – activities that were light years away from what we were doing; but what was so extraordinary was that those girls were being educated by nuns. They were 'good Catholic girls' and yet they were leading a life that seemed to me to be open, sunny, glorious, free and full of ego-boosting activities. I couldn't reconcile my dark, dark, miserable 'Tom Brown' schooldays with those glorious sunny schooldays in Los Angeles. Maybe if I went back properly into my schooldays I might find that there was happiness, as there was in the hay shed, but those yearbooks were certainly a leap for me into the future. They gave me the determination to leave my darkness behind and to get into an inch of space that was sunny for myself.

The Run of His Library

Writer and literary critic, DENIS DONOGHUE, grew up in Warrenpoint, Co. Down, where access to a neighbour's library sparked his early interest in literary criticism.

I went to the local Catholic school, St Peter's, a small three-teacher school. One of the teachers, Sean Crawford, a rather remarkable and genial character, lived a few doors from us, just in the square. We had the run of the Crawfords' house. I formed with him and his daughter a little trio and we used to play music. Even more to the point, he was a literary person who made available to me his small but fairly select library. In my family we had no books at all of the slightest significance. Apart from schoolbooks, I recall only one book in the house and that was a book my father had called *A Guide to Careers*, which indeed was a very useful book. When I wanted something to read, I would go through Sean Crawford's collection of books, so the beginnings of my readings were done with the aid of his library. It had the standard works of English fiction – Jane Austen, George Eliot, and so on. There was a magazine at the time called *John O'London's Weekly* and he had a very large, bound volume, an entire year's issue. I think what first started my interest in literary criticism was this bound volume, because, in addition to stories, it had several critical essays by people like Robert Lynd and Frank Swinnerton, who were men of letters at the time. I got my first introduction to what it was to write a formal essay and perhaps even to have it published through *John O'London's Weekly* because these were civilised English essays that had a beginning, a middle and an end, in that order.

Sean Crawford used to write little essays and little squibs for the *Irish Press*. He was a strange, angular and rather daft individual, but extraordinarily humane. I remember him vividly as a teacher, not in terms of anything very tangible he taught me but in the sense that he really made it clear to me that there was a larger world out there that was full of all kinds of magical things: novels and poems and music.

Hooked on Books

Like many parents, writer ANNE FINE tried hard to get her children interested in reading, but she discovered that there is no sure-fire way. You never can tell what will hook a child.

———

My own younger daughter was, at the age of eight, not a reader. Oh, she could read, but she didn't, not often. She spent hours on her hand-held computer games, and she made things, and she rode her bike. She was, as it happens, educated in an American kindergarten and elementary school, and there, the textbooks had all been rewritten to show girls poring over engines and boys counting up buttons. There had been, throughout California, a concerted effort to eradicate institutionalised sexism from the school system. We came back to Britain and visited my mother, who promptly handed me three cartons of my old Enid Blyton books. 'Here,' she said 'take them or they go to the jumble sale.' Now,

Enid Blyton is not exactly what a mother who sees herself as much on the front line of feminism as the next man wants to take home to a houseful of impressionable daughters! But I really did love these books when I was young, and I could never have let them go for jumble. So they were stacked on the back seat of the car and we set off for home in Edinburgh. And all the way up the M1 and the M6, and the A74, and the M8, we could hear this bitter little eight-year-old voice spluttering and muttering from the back seat. 'Of course the boys are going through the hedge first ... of course ... of course it's the girls that are crying ... of course ... of course it's the girls who have to make the sandwiches ... of course ... of course it's the boys who get to fetch the boat.' By the time we reached home, my daughter was spitting poison with Enid Blyton's sexism, and she was on her *sixth* book. And from that day to this, my daughter has been the most passionate reader.

My First Book

JOAN LINGARD grew up in Belfast and is another writer who was obsessed with books. A chance remark by her mother started Joan's writing career at the age of eleven.

———

I was absolutely crazy about books. They fascinated me. I could never get enough to read and I am sure that is why I ultimately became a writer. The local library was quite far away, so I couldn't go there on my own when I was young. It appeared to me then to be like an old shed; and, in fact, when I went back there again recently it still looked like that! The books then were very tattered and ancient. They had long since lost their dust jackets and their spines had a greasy feeling about them. The pages were filthy, spattered with egg and tomato ketchup. I hated the feel of those books so much that I used to turn the pages with a postcard and cover the spine with a paper wrapper – but that didn't thwart my love of the books themselves. I read absolutely everything I was allowed to read in the junior library – you weren't allowed into the senior section until you were fourteen. I read all the books that children have loved for years – the 'Chalet School' books, Enid Blyton, *Just William, Biggles* – and when my mother would ask me what I wanted for Christmas I always demanded a book. One Christmas I got eight books and I had read them all before I went to bed that night! My mother was beginning to despair of keeping me supplied with books and finally one day, when I was moaning, 'I've got nothing to read, I'm bored!', she turned to me and said, 'Why don't you go away and write your own books?' That was how I began as a writer, at the age of eleven.

I got some lined foolscap paper, filled my fountain pen with green ink (because I thought that was a very suitable colour for a writer!) and sat down to write my first book. It was about a girl call Gail. It was one of those books in which a telegram arrives calling the parents away to somewhere like Rangoon ('Great Aunt Emily very ill. Come at once!'). Gail was sent to her grandmother in

Cornwall where she found a smugglers' cave which led to various secret passages ... Eventually she tracked down the smugglers and was confronted by a villain with scars zigzagging down his face to the corners of his mouth. It was very unsubtle characterisation: he might as well have had a placard on his chest saying, 'I am the villain!' In the end, Gail brings the smugglers to justice and – lo and behold! – her uncle Bill appears on the scene and he happens to be a detective who has been trying to track the smugglers down for years without success. There were definitely shades of Enid Blyton lurking in the background!

I wasn't happy with my 'book' in loose sheets. I wanted to make a real book, so I copied the whole story out in my best writing in an exercise book (in blue ink this time). I made a dust-wrapper, illustrated it and wrote a 'blurb'. I wrote 'Books by Joan Lingard' on the back, then under it 'No. 1 – *Gail*' and at the bottom, 'Published by Lingard & Co.' That was my first publication.

Other books were to follow in this series, 'Books by Joan Lingard'. I wrote *The Further Adventures of*

Gail and another book was *The Strange House on the Moors*. The latter was a story about twin girls of fourteen and it was set on the Yorkshire moors. I remember painting the twins on the cover. They had long blonde hair in plaits down to the waist. (There was a certain amount of wish-fulfilment in that: I had always wanted to grow my hair long but my mother wouldn't allow it, in case I picked up lice in school. She insisted on a pudding-bowl style.) The twins arrived on the moors on a wild, stormy night and a big mansion loomed up before them. The door opened and an evil-looking housekeeper invited them in – I think that by then I would have been reading the Brontës!

The Beginning of
A VOCATION

———

'I was opened up to the whole world of the poor,
the broken, the "losers" of humanity.'

MY FATHER'S AFFAIRS

In the teeming city of Jerusalem, crowds assemble to celebrate the Passover. Among them, a twelve-year-old boy, who goes missing.

———

Every year the parents of Jesus used to go to Jerusalem for the feast of the Passover. When he was twelve years old, they went up for the feast as usual. When they were on their way home after the feast, the boy Jesus stayed behind in Jerusalem without his parents knowing it. They assumed he was with the caravan, and it was only after a day's journey that they went to look for him among their relations and acquaintances. When they failed to find him, they went back to Jerusalem looking for him everywhere.

Three days later, they found him in the Temple, sitting among the doctors, listening to them, and asking them questions; and all those who heard him were astounded at his intelligence and his replies. They were overcome when they saw him, and his mother said to him, 'My child, why have you done this to us? See how worried your father and I have been, looking for you.' 'Why were you looking for me?' he replied. 'Did you not know that I must be busy with my Father's affairs?' But they did not understand what he meant.

He then went down with them and came to Nazareth and lived under their authority. His mother stored up all these things in her heart. And Jesus increased in wisdom, in stature and in favour with God and men.

Luke 2:41–52

A Nun Takes the Veil

Two perspectives on this major undertaking. First a poet's view from GERARD MANLEY HOPKINS. Then the actual experience of a Carmelite sister, MARY BRIGEEN WILSON from the city of Derry.

Heaven – Haven

A nun takes the veil

I have desired to go
Where springs not fail,
To fields where flies no sharp and sided hail
And a few lilies blow.

And I have asked to be
Where no storms come,
Where the green swell is in the havens dumb,
And out of the swing of the sea.

The Beginning of a Vocation / 219

My name is Sr Mary Brigeen Wilson, and I live in a happy community of ten sisters here in our Monastery of St Joseph, Kilmacud, Co. Dublin. Our ages range from thirty-six to ninety years and that includes two lovely young Vietnamese sisters, who have come to us for a few years to learn English and experience Carmelite life in a different culture. They have brought us much joy and an injection of new life! We also have two of our dear elderly sisters being cared for in local nursing homes. They are a vital part of our community; our little 'diaspora'. We visit them regularly, keeping our family bonds strong and alive. We are blessed to have a young Irish girl discerning her vocation with us at this time.

Growing up in Derry in the fifties and sixties with my devoted hard-working parents and seven siblings was a privileged experience of family life, and a great preparation for life in community. We learned to love and watch out for each other, to value work and to make sacrifices, to be grateful for what we had and to share with those who had less. We had the usual childhood squabbles and skirmishes but learnt to make up and forgive. We were blessed with a big extended family; three of our grandparents and a large circle of aunts, uncles and cousins lived near us. As a 'clan' we went on holidays to my maternal grandmother's home in Ballyliffin, Inishowen.

Those were magical years that are fresh and green in my memory still. I loved the sea and the wide-open vistas, the simplicity of life, the rugged beauty and peace, running around in my bare feet, and climbing the hills of Donegal. I loved the communal dips, picnics and fancy dresses. The power and immensity of the ocean spoke to me of God and things eternal, and I have no doubt that all this sowed in my heart the seeds of my contemplative vocation.

My whole childhood and youth were steeped in our Catholic faith. It was interwoven into everyday life and influenced all that we thought and did. It gave a sense of security and hope, and God's provident care kept our hearts trusting and peaceful.

Prayer was a vital part of our home, morning and evening; the family Rosary, grace at meals, etc.

Prayer was as natural as breathing, passed on to us in word and example by our wonderful parents. The Sacred Heart wasn't only a picture, but a real 'presence' in our kitchen, as Mammy spoke of him and to him with such naturalness. The saints were our good friends. As we grew older, we attended morning Mass with Daddy, vying with each other to link arms with him on the short trip to the church.

I attended St Columba's, Long Tower, in the heart of Derry city, the oldest Catholic church in the city and built near the site of Columba's original monastery. Every year his feast was preceded by a novena that was very well attended and on the actual feast there was outdoor Mass in Irish. In preparation for the big day, the church and little houses nearby would get a facelift. There would be a great spate of painting and scrubbing up; bunting, flags and banners would be brought out for yet another year and everyone sang out the hymn to St Columba with great pride and gusto.

Looking back, it seems that there was a great 'faith culture' in the city. This was certainly very evident in the yearly retreats. Every May the whole city of Derry went on retreat, each parish having its own preachers; the women and girls for the first week and the men and boys for the second. We used to get up for the 6 a.m. Mass and when we came home and had our breakfast (many of the early Mass-goers called in to the local bakery for the traditional Derry 'baps', fresh from the oven), we were glad of the stretch of time to revise for exams before heading for school. At the close of the week the ladies would step out 'in their figures' in their new clothes while the men all wore a little flower in their lapels, as at weddings. I remember so well that a dear Protestant friend always supplied Daddy's flower, usually lily of the valley or narcissus grown in the local allotments or 'plots'. We were always touched by that gesture, and it indicates the good relationship we had with our Protestant neighbours. Every Sunday we attended devotions, usually with Daddy as Mammy was engaged at home with the current baby. Years later my younger sister told me that she always thought the monstrance sang, because beautiful music would begin when it appeared. What a lovely memory from a child's innocent heart!

While I always felt the call to contemplative life, my journey of discernment led me to the Sisters of Mercy for some years. God's hand was in it as I never forget the wonderful training I received and an introduction to the vibrant Mercy charism rich in compassion and humanity. It was a learning experience to go on visitation to the homes and hospitals with a senior sister companion and to witness first-hand the trials and poverty of many families. I got the opportunity to go to Queen's University, and to teach for a year in an Intermediate school in the disadvantaged Creggan area in Derry. I loved the spontaneity of the children, their affection and resilient joy amid great hardship. Even though I loved what I was doing at every stage, the call to Carmel would surface again and again ...

Those were the early years of the Troubles and it was heart-breaking to see the havoc they wrought: families broken and scarred for life with the untimely death of loved ones; young people caught up in the violence; homes and family businesses destroyed; and soaring unemployment. I am grateful that God let me experience these things because they made my prayer more real when I came to Carmel. More than ever I felt I could best help to heal this great yawning wound of my people by a life of prayer. Like St Thérèse, I felt the call to be 'love in the heart of the Church'. And so, when the time seemed right I transferred to Carmel; this time leaving two families: my natural family and Mercy family. But it wasn't a leaving, for I carried them both in my heart with great love and gratitude. I never regret God's vocational journey for me; my personal 'salvation history'.

St Thérèse's vision for her small reformed Carmels was that of a family where the sisters would be friends; loving, cherishing and helping one another. The Holy Spirit creates out of a very mixed bag of individuals of all ages and backgrounds, talents and temperaments, a communion of hearts and minds, a warm family spirit. We don't leave our human nature at the monastery gate. There's no getting away from it! Our humanity is still flawed, still in travail; we are a work in process. Often, as the day ends, a deep sense of gratitude sweeps over me as I look at each of my sisters in all their vulnerability and hidden heroic efforts; the sheer beauty of human life; the privilege of walking the road together, rubbing shoulders with these 'saints in the making'. Yes, it is good to be here, to be on the road together, to be that bit nearer *home*.

Beautiful People

JEAN VANIER came from a very comfortable background. Educated in England and Canada, he was teaching philosophy in Paris when he was introduced to a group of men with mental disabilities – a meeting that changed Jean's life.

———

I went to visit them with much fear and some misgivings, because I didn't know how to communicate with people who had a mental handicap. How do you speak with people who can't speak? And even if they did speak, what would we talk about? I was very touched by these men with all that was broken in them, their handicaps, their incapacities. Each was asking, 'Do you love me? Will you be my friend?' My students in philosophy wanted my head but not my heart. They were interested in the courses I could give them so that they could pass their exams and move on. They were not saying, 'Do you love me?' They were saying, 'What can you give me to pass my exam?'

I loved teaching, but it was not really my purpose in life. I was seeking my life's work, not just a job. In the navy, and then in the world of studies, I had been in the world of the strong, the 'winners'. Here, I was opened up to the whole world of the poor, the broken, the 'losers' of humanity. I was touched by their cry and by their terrible situations.

The First Sign

JESUS CHRIST sets out on his mission.

———

There was a wedding at Cana in Galilee. The mother of Jesus was there, and Jesus and his disciples had also been invited. When they ran out of wine, since the wine provided for the wedding was all finished, the mother of Jesus said to him, 'They have no wine.' Jesus said, 'Woman, why turn to me? My hour has not come yet.' His mother said to the servants, 'Do whatever he tells you.' There were six stone water jars standing there, meant for the ablutions that are customary among the Jews: each could hold twenty or thirty gallons. Jesus said to the servants, 'Fill the jars with water.' And they filled them to the brim. 'Draw some out now', he told them, 'and take it to the steward.' They did this; the steward tasted the water, and it had turned into wine. Having no idea where it came from – only the servants who had drawn the water knew – the steward called the bridegroom and said, 'People generally serve the best wine first, and keep the cheaper sort till the guests have had plenty to drink; but you have kept the best wine till now.'

This was the first of the signs given by Jesus: it was given at Cana in Galilee. He let his glory be seen, and his disciples believed in him.

John 2:1–11

SEVENTY YEARS IN THE VINEYARD

NORMAN DAVITT is a missionary with the Divine Word Missionaries (SVD) who came to his vocation very early. He was born in Birmingham in March 1921, of Irish lineage. His grandfather came from Ballyhaunis, Co. Mayo. In 2017, he celebrated seventy years in the priesthood.

———

I was the second of five boys. My father would not have been a strong Catholic, but he said his private prayers daily and went to Mass on Sunday. My mother was a convert to Catholicism and was a daily Mass-goer when she could, taking me with her.

I'm not sure where the seeds of a vocation came from, but they were probably influenced by the stories of African missionaries. At any rate, a priest visited our school when I was nine and asked us what we would like to be when we grew up. Without giving it any thought, my reply was 'a missionary'. Two years later he asked us again and I gave the same reply. He gave me a missal and recommended daily Mass. Later he summoned me to his house to meet a small man with a big beard. 'This is Fr King,' he explained. 'He works in China with the Divine Word Missionaries. They are opening a new college in Droitwich [outside Birmingham]. Do you want to go?' 'Yes,' I replied. My father was very much against the idea, but my mother persuaded him and so it was that in September 1933 he put me on the bus to Droitwich with my little suitcase. I was twelve years old.

The young age didn't bother me. Many others got homesick and left, but I was content enough. It was what was known as a 'minor seminary', a sort of pre-novitiate. A boy called Tony Fleming had joined a year before me and ultimately, he and I were the only two that survived from those two groups. Six years later I was watching a cricket match one day when my mother arrived waving a telegram. 'Proceed at once to Donamon,' it said. Donamon Castle in Co. Roscommon was the order's house in Ireland – where I live now – so we students were given money to get the ferry to Dublin and travel from there to Donamon. We arrived on 3 September 1939, the day World War II broke out. The irony was that Donamon was staffed by German priests, so while my brothers went off to fight the Germans in the war, I was living at peace with Germans in an Irish castle! There was no unease in that for me. I loved the Irish countryside and spent three years in the novitiate before returning to England to study philosophy. When the war was over Tony and I were sent to America 'to get the true spirit of the SVD' and we were finally ordained there on 15 August 1947.

I was sent on vocations work for three years in England and Ireland before achieving my ultimate goal – working with tribal peoples in India, travelling on foot and by motorbike through the paddy fields, bringing the faith to those lovely people. I travelled huge distances. What was once my 'parish' is now a diocese! Eight years later I came home for a refresher course in Rome but instead of returning I was sent back to England to be the regional superior. This was not my scene at all and I made that known! I wanted missionary work and eventually Rome relented and I was sent to Papua New Guinea, a country which I knew little about but where I would minister for nearly thirty years. I began on the coast but contracted cerebral malaria there. My doctor told me to move to the highlands, where the climate was better. The people were warrior tribes whose leaders practised polygamy but they were very welcoming to me. The 'training' I had got didn't prepare me for this at all. All I really needed was the Bible, a strong faith and a practical approach to life and it worked out well in the end. I did my job of converting and building up the faith. For a time, I worked in Abullua, which was so remote that I had to be dropped in by helicopter, but I loved the work and the people. My prayer life was the Mass, the Divine Office and a holy hour on my own every evening (something I still practise).

All through my missionary life, it was Jesus that energised me. He spread the Word and let people decide. He didn't force anyone in or out. When I celebrated my seventieth year as a priest, a quote in the celebratory Mass booklet summed up my credo, 'I have not lost confidence, because I know what it is that I put my trust in. I have no doubt at all that he is able to take care of all I have entrusted to him.' And in some strange way, I seemed to know that at nine years of age.

In the End is the
BEGINNING

———

'The sun rises in spite of everything.'

Begin Again

Losing a loved one suddenly is a very hard blow. I know. It happened to me on 25 June 2001 when my beautiful wife, Olive, died while swimming in the sea off Rosslare Strand in Co. Wexford. Nothing can prepare you for such an event. The goalposts have been moved. Life will never be the same again, but life has to go on. You must begin again. In my case, part of the beginning was to resume writing to Olive. Nobody recommended it. It just seemed obvious, as letters had played a major part in our courtship. The following was written in October 2001, some four months after Olive had died.

My darling,
They say it's good to write, so here goes. It's entirely

appropriate anyway. Thirty-five years ago, I courted you by letter. We were patients in a TB sanatorium and the day I saw this vision in a black leather coat I was smitten!

It was 1 March 1966 and a few days later I put pen to paper. Tentative first step! As for the postal system within the sanatorium – we were dependent on a friendly nurse or porter to smuggle letters from one unit to another. Just like boarding school! What a way to treat twenty-somethings – but it worked.

And then the waiting. And then the reply! We were up and running! The letters continued. Wonderful, wonderful letters that brightened up long boring days, weeks, months. Wonderful, wonderful letters where we gradually unfolded our personalities and slowly learned about each other.

Do you remember the Bank Holiday Monday when we went for a walk, slipped away through the woods and walked around the sanatorium boiler house seventeen times? Exotic or what? It was the most wonderful day of my life up to then. I was in love.

What you saw in me then I do not know, but thank you for all seventeen laps. And thank you for replying to that first letter. It was meant to be. Little did either of us think on entering the sanatorium that we would meet our life partner. Two and a half years later we married. It was meant to be. Thank you, my love.

A few weeks after your death I came across those first letters again. I had kept yours in a biscuit tin for thirty-five years and never looked at them. I suppose I knew there would be a day ... I was delighted to find that you had kept some of my letters too. I read them in tears, and just fell in love with you all over again. It was a beautiful feeling. I walked on air just as I had all those years ago. Everything was possible. Nothing was a problem, except for one thing: you were no longer physically present. But the wonderful innocence of those letters, the gentle unfolding of those personalities, the gradual realisation of love. Thank you. Again.

It hasn't been all joy, of course. Far from it. The emptiness, the loneliness. And the regrets. If only I had done this, hadn't done that, had said this, hadn't said that … I *know* it's wrong to be like that. All the textbooks, all the counsellors tell you not to think like that. I know. But I'm human.

And I know they weren't thirty-three years of unending bliss (far from it, I hear you sigh!). Arguments, disagreements, rows. Irritation. Exasperation. All the 'stuff' that got in the way. Money problems, health problems. Worries over children. Life! We stuck at it. The foundations were solid. It was meant to be.

That's why I tell couples now to cherish the arguments and the rows. They are part of the warp and woof of married life. I know it's hard to see it at the time, but believe me, the scales have been lifted from my eyes. I can see clearly now. For putting up with my stubbornness, selfishness, stupidity, thank you, my love.

And, of course, it wasn't all black! We had wonderful times, memorable days, deeply cherished moments. Just look at the photographs (how I cherish them now). The laughter, the smiles, the memories. And not always the big occasions. Very often it's the little things.

John O'Donohue has put it beautifully, 'The kingdom of memory is full of the ruins of presence.' … His writings have been a great consolation to me over the past four months (or is it centuries?). He also quotes Meister Eckhart in maintaining that the souls of the dead don't 'go' anywhere. They are here with us, all the time, 'You can sense the presence of those you love who have died. With the refinement of your soul, you can sense them. You feel that they are near.'

I'll second that. I believe in your 'presence'. That's why I talk to you all the time ('Much more than you did when I was here,' I hear you sigh). That's why I write to you every night (You see I'm still courting you!). The damburst in my heart has released the most intimate outpourings.

That's why I recognise you in St Stephen's Green, four weeks after you died. There I was, sitting on a bench remembering a lovely evening a year ago when we sat on a bench in the green, just enjoying the loveliness and contentment of it all … There I was with my memories when I was accosted by a down-and-out who proceeded to tell me his life story. A former jockey who fell foul of the racing law, hit the bottle, lost his home, marriage broke up, now living rough … A most engaging fellow, not in any way obnoxious.

I thought to myself – Olive would love this guy, knowing her feeling for the downtrodden. I gave him a few bob and stood up to go. For some reason I told him how I had lost you suddenly a month earlier. He put his arms around me, whispered in my ear – 'The seed in your heart shall blossom' – and walked away.

I was totally stunned. When I looked back he waved to me and mimed that sentence again. Weird! Wonderful! We talk of drink, gambling, broken marriage, etc. and then he comes out with this poetry.

Only then did I realise that it was you or your angel – had to be. I'm totally convinced of that. And of course, you/he were right. The seed in my heart has blossomed, wonderfully, beautifully – and continues to blossom. Thank you, my darling.

Let nobody think it's easy though. It's a hard and lonely road and ultimately, it's a road you walk alone. *I miss you!* Terribly. Frighteningly. You were so much part of the fabric of my life.

Only now do I realise that you were truly and literally my 'other half' and that with your going a great part of me has gone too. And I owe you so much – and never told you how much! Well I'm telling you now. You made me the person I am. My real date of birth was 1 March 1966. Do I make myself clear? *I need you.* Now more than ever. So, stay very close to me, please. Or else I shall fall apart.

> Love you. Miss you. Above all, thank you.
> John
> (29 October 2001)

The End – or the Beginning?

In the concluding pages of his mammoth autobiography, Long Walk to Freedom, *NELSON MANDELA realises that the ending of his lifetime-long walk is only a beginning.*

———

It was during those long and lonely years that my hunger for the freedom of my own people became a hunger for the freedom of all people, white and black. I knew as well as I knew anything that the oppressor must be liberated just as surely as the oppressed. A man who takes away another man's freedom is a prisoner of hatred, he is locked behind the bars of prejudice and narrow-mindedness. I am not truly free if I am taking away someone else's freedom, just as surely as I am not free when my freedom is taken from me. The oppressed and the oppressor alike are robbed of their humanity.

When I walked out of prison, that was my mission, to liberate the oppressed and the oppressor both. Some say that has now been achieved. But I know that that is not the case. The truth is that we are not yet free; we have merely achieved the freedom to be free, the right not to be oppressed. We have not taken the final step of our journey, but the first step on a longer and even more difficult road. For to be free is not merely to cast off one's chains, but to live in a way that respects and enhances the freedom of others. The true test of our devotion to freedom is just beginning.

I have walked that long road to freedom. I have tried not to falter; I have made missteps along the way. But I have discovered the secret that after climbing a great hill, one only finds that there are many more hills to climb. I have taken a moment here to rest, to steal a view of the glorious vista that surrounds me, to look back on the distance I have come. But I can rest only for a moment, for with freedom comes responsibilities, and I dare not linger, for my long walk is not yet ended.

The Clouds Clearing

To end the beginnings, some positive uplifting lines from the pen of DEREK MAHON.

—

Everything Is Going to Be All Right

How should I not be glad to contemplate
the clouds clearing beyond the dormer window
and a high tide reflected on the ceiling?
There will be dying, there will be dying,
but there is no need to go into that.
The lines flow from the hand unbidden
and the hidden source is the watchful heart;
the sun rises in spite of everything
and the far cities are beautiful and bright.
I lie here in a riot of sunlight
watching the day break and the clouds flying.
Everything is going to be all right.

Epilogue

In the Beginning

In the beginning was the Word
But the Word was not the beginning.
When the light faded
On the gestures of order
Fired at unbroken time
The pieces descending
Into darkness
Did not arrange themselves
Except in arbitrary shape.

Nor was the beginning out of order.
Nor was the word that sought order the beginning.
The word was an arbitrary shape
Beyond gaze and breath.
It was in glorious darkness

Out of Chaos
The Word came.

That first scream of need
Is the beginning
Of a long surrender
That is not easily borne.
The struggle for a recovered silence
Will never be complete.
That look that precedes the word
Will stay to haunt.
The breath that interceded
Will break forth at times
In a great scream of grief or love.

And, if in weakness
We polish the wild words
To make a prayerful set of beads
From the jagged edges of stony times,
Or cry out on a Sunday shadow sated,
Then sing our souls
Not for the fading of the light
Nor yet the ebbing sea.

Through tears,
It is a worn face.
Not white
But ebony,
We seek
Calling from the darkness
Before the Word
And the false promise of order.

The salt of tears
Is a deposit in memory
Of our sea beginnings.
There is lodged
The long sigh
Of all our time
Lost in endless space.

President Michael D. Higgins

Sources

The Beginning of Life: William Blake, 'Infant Joy' from *Songs of Innocence*, 1789, and 'The Angel That Presided O'er My Birth' from 'Epigrams, Verses, and Fragments from The Note-Book (*c.*1808–11)' in G. Keynes, *Complete Writings with Variant Readings*, Oxford: Oxford University Press, 1966. Seamus Heaney, radio interview with John Quinn. Thomas Hood, 'I Remember, I Remember', *Poets of the English Language*, New York: Viking Press, 1950. Walt Whitman, 'There Was a Child Went Forth', *Leaves of Grass*, 1855. Patrick Kavanagh, 'The Long Garden', Antoinette Quinn (ed.), *Collected Poems*, Allen Lane, 2004. The Beginning of Learning: Isaac Stern, 'Music and the Child' in *The Curious Mind: Twenty-five Years of John Quinn Radio Programmes*, Dublin: Veritas, 2009, pp. 263–4. Mike Cooley, Open Mind Guest Lecture, 1989. Shinichi Suzuki, *Nurtured by Love: the Classic Approach to Talent Education*, Waltraud Suzuki (tr.), USA: Alfred Publishing Co., Inc., 1983. Seamus Heaney in Dennis O'Driscoll, *Stepping Stones: Interviews with Seamus Heaney*, London: Faber & Faber, 2008, p. 17. Elizabeth Shane, 'Wee Hughie', *Collected Poems*, Dundalgan Press, 1945. Kornei Chukovsky, *From Two to Five*, Miriam Morton (tr. and ed.), Berkeley: University of California Press, 1971, p. 10. Ben Zander, radio interview with John Quinn. James Plunkett, in John Quinn (ed.), *Must Try Harder: Tales Out of School from Sixty Well-known Personalities*, 1985. The Beginning of Love: Ewan MacColl and

Peggy Seeger, radio interview with John Quinn. Maeve Binchy, in John Quinn (ed.), *A Portrait of the Artist as a Young Girl*, London: Methuen, 1986. Robert Burns, 'When First I Saw'. **The Beginning of a Dream:** Sacha Abercorn (ed.), *Sourcing Voices*, Omagh: Pushkin Trust, 2014. Maeve Binchy, in *A Portrait*. WB Yeats, 'The Lake Isle of Innisfree', *The Collected Poems of WB Yeats*, Hertfordshire: Wordsworth Poetry Library, 2000, p. 31. Eugene Clarke, radio documentary by John Quinn; Henry Ford, *My Life and Work*, Doubleday, 1922. John Quinn, *Letters to Olive: Sea of Love, Sea of Loss: Seed of Love, Seed of Life*, Dublin: Veritas, 2011. **The Beginning of a Career:** Johnny McDaid, in *Sourcing Voices*. John B. Keane, in *Must Try Harder*. Jennifer Johnston, in *A Portrait*. Cyril Cusack, Jimmy Magee, and Spike Milligan, in *Must Try Harder*. Feargal Quinn, in John Quinn, *My Education*, Dublin: Town House, 1997. Dervla Murphy, in *A Portrait*. Éamonn Mac Thomais, in *Must Try Harder*. Peter Ustinov, radio interview with John Quinn. Mary Lavin, in *A Portrait*. **The Beginning of a New Time:** Michael Coady, 'The Blind Poet's Vision of Spring', *Given Light*, Oldcastle: The Gallery Press, 2017, p. 38. William Wordsworth, 'Composed upon Westminster Bridge, September 3, 1802', *Poems in Two Volumes*, London: Longman, Hurst, Rees, and Orme, 1807. Francis Ledwidge, 'June', in Alice Curtayne (ed.), *Francis Ledwidge: Complete Poems*, London: Martin Brian & O'Keefe, 1974. Jenny Joseph, 'Warning', in *Selected Poems*, Bloodaxe Books, 1992. **The Beginning of Wisdom:** Tony O'Reilly, in *My Education*; Rudyard Kipling, 'If', *A Choice of Kipling's Verse*, New York: Scribner, 1943. Noam Chomsky, and John Seymour, in *My Education*. Frank McCourt, *Teacher Man*, London: Fourth Estate, 2005. **The Beginning of Hope:** Donie O'Sullivan, in Brian Carthy, *Football Captains: The All-Ireland Winners*, Dublin:

Wolfhound Press, 1993. John Hume, Open Mind Guest Lecture, 1994. Brendan Kennelly, 'Begin', *Familiar Strangers: New & Selected Poems 1960–2004*, Bloodaxe Books, 2004. George Mitchell, Open Mind Guest Lecture, 1998. Ken Whitaker, radio interview with John Quinn; William Wordsworth, 'The French Revolution as It Appeared to Enthusiasts at Its Commencement', *The Complete Poetical Works*, London: Macmillan and Co., 1888. **The Beginning of a Journey:** Charles Handy, *My Education*. John F. Deane, *Must Try Harder*. Ashley Beck, *Dorothy Day*, London: CTS; Francis Thompson, 'The Hound of Heaven', in DHS Nicholson and AHE Lee (eds.), *The Oxford Book of English Mystical Verse*, Oxford: The Clarendon Press, 1917. **A Beginning with Books:** Polly Devlin, *A Portrait*. Denis Donoghue, *My Education*. Anne Fine, Open Mind Guest Lecture, 1996. **The Beginning of a Vocation:** Gerard Manley Hopkins, 'Heaven – Haven', *Poems of Gerard Manley Hopkins*, Robert Bridges (ed.), London: Humphrey Milford, 1918; Mary Brigeen Wilson, personal letter. Jean Vanier, *My Education*. Norman Davitt, interview with John Quinn, 2017. **In the End is the Beginning:** Nelson Mandela, *Long Walk to Freedom*, London: Abacus, 1994. Derek Mahon, 'Everything Is Going to Be All Right', *New Selected Poems*, Oldcastle: The Gallery Press, 2015. **Epilogue:** Michael D. Higgins, 'In the Beginning', *An Arid Season: New Poems*, Dublin: New Island, 2004.